AF538408

ALSO BY SUSAN KALISH

Pattern Design for Needlepoint and Patchwork
Oriental Rugs in Needlepoint

PILLOW TALK

SUSAN KALISH

SIMON AND SCHUSTER | NEW YORK

TEXT BY NANCY KALISH

Published by Simon and Schuster
A Division of Simon & Schuster, Inc.
Simon & Schuster Building
Rockefeller Center
1230 Avenue of the Americas
New York, New York 10020
SIMON AND SCHUSTER and colophon
are registered trademarks of Simon & Schuster, Inc.
Designed by Edith Fowler
Manufactured in the United States of America

10 9 8 7 6 5 4 3 2 1

Library of Congress Cataloging in Publication Data

Kalish, Susan Schoenfeld.
Pillow talk.

1. Canvas embroidery—Patterns. 2. Quotations.
3. Pillows. I. Kalish, Nancy. II. Title.
TT778.C3K355 1985 746.9 85-14204
ISBN 0-671-54565-5

ACKNOWLEDGMENTS

Woody Allen:	*Those who can, do. Those who can't, teach. Those who can't teach, teach gym.*
Yogi Berra:	*It ain't over till it's over.*
Charlie Brown:	*No problem is so big or so complicated that it can't be run away from.*
Dwight Eisenhower:	*Things today are more like they've ever been.*
King Lear:	*HA!*
Jacob Kalish:	*Homework gives me a rash.*
Muriel Kalish:	*God loves women with fat thighs.*
Steve Martin:	*A day without sunshine is . . . like night.*
Mae West:	*Too much of a good thing is wonderful.*

And thanks to all the other funny people whose words appear in this collection.

CONTENTS

INTRODUCTION

I began doing needlepoint when I was nine and had pneumonia. I was so sick that I was taken out of school and sent from Brooklyn to New Jersey to recover under the care of my grandmother.

Terribly bored, and quickly running out of diversions, I gave in one day and learned the needlepoint stitches my grandmother had been wanting to show me. By the end of the month, I had completed my first project—a needlepoint pillow. It read, of course, "I love Grandma."

I found out then that one of the quickest ways to a person's heart may be through a personalized needlepoint saying, and I have been designing and making them ever since.

This book will show you how to combine the words of such greats as Woody Allen, Mae West, Dwight Eisenhower, King Lear, and 101 others with the colors of your choice and stitch your way to personalized and professional-looking pillows for friends and family or to rest on your own favorite easy chair.

Friends already acquainted with the joys of stitching will also appreciate the gift of a custom-made needlepoint kit, worth from fifty to two hundred dollars, that you can make yourself for just a few dollars by following the instructions in this book. You only pay for the cost of the materials and a pretty basket or box in which to place them.

All the projects in this book are quick, inexpensive, and easy to make. The materials you use are widely available, and everything you need to know from your first stitch to your last is included in straightforward and simple instructions.

But you'd better watch out. Needlepoint has a relaxing rhythm that's almost addictive. Pick it up to blast away boredom or the blues, or just to keep your hands out of the refrigerator when you're dieting.

And you'll find that when pillows talk, people listen. The sayings in this book will no doubt help you face reality—"A person's nose and ears continue to grow throughout his or her lifetime"; deal with problems—"When the going gets tough, the tough go shopping"; celebrate life's consolations—"I love champagne, caviar, and cash"; or simply express yourself—"I watch the Phil Donahue Show."

Read all the instructions through from beginning to end, then practice the stitches a bit before starting a pillow; you'll find the projects in this book both easy and entertaining.

Just remember, "He who laughs, lasts."

Happy stitching!

WHAT YOU WILL NEED

- Canvas
- Needles
- Yarn
- Thimble
- Scissors
- Masking Tape
- Ruler
- Permanent waterproof markers
- White acrylic paint
- Small paintbrush
- Plant sprayer
- Homosote board
- Brown wrapping paper
- Rustproof pushpins
- White glue
- Muslin
- Sewing thread
- Dacron stuffing
- Backing material

CANVAS

Needlepoint canvas is a stiff cotton fabric, loosely woven to create holes of equal size between threads. The resulting mesh looks a lot like window screening. Available at crafts and fabric stores, needlepoint canvas is sold by the yard and comes in many different gauges.

The gauge is determined by the number of threads per inch of the canvas. No. 10 canvas has ten threads per inch. No. 12 canvas has twelve threads per inch. All the patterns in this book were designed for 10 gauge canvas, but you can make them smaller or larger by simply using a different gauge.

There are two types of needlepoint canvas. Mono mesh is woven with a single thread in each direction. Penelope is woven with two threads in each direction.

For the projects in this book, I recommend using No. 10 white cotton mono mesh canvas. It is the easiest to stitch, is the most durable, and produces the best-looking needlepoint.

But no matter what type of canvas you use, you must always bind the edges so that they don't unravel. To do this, fold a piece of one-inch-wide masking tape over each edge.

Half a yard of mono mesh canvas (one yard wide) will make six to eight pillows, with some left over to practice on.

You can also buy a plastic mesh, which is better for making items such as wall hangings, tote bags, place mats, and boxes. This plastic canvas comes in precut sheets or by the yard. When using a precut sheet, make sure it has enough threads to accommodate the saying you have chosen.

The sayings in this book can also be worked sampler style on cloth, using the cross-stitch. For this method, use embroidery thread and a No. 22 tapestry needle, and do the design only on even-weave cloth (a cloth with no visible holes, but with very evenly woven threads that you can count).

NEEDLES

For your needlepoint, you should use tapestry needles with a blunt point and a large eye. They come in assorted sizes, but use a No. 18 needle on 10 and 12 gauge mono mesh.

When using a different gauge of mesh, remember that the larger the holes, the larger the needle you must use. The number of the needle size goes down as the needle gets larger.

YARN

No matter how gorgeous the color of the yarn, your needlepoint won't look very pretty unless the yarn has covered the canvas completely. None of the white mesh should show through.

The yarn must be strong enough to take the repeated wear of being pulled through the canvas, and so you should never use any yarns except those made especially for needlepoint tapestry.

I recommend using Persian yarn with No. 10 mono mesh for stitching the sayings in this book. Persian yarn has three strands loosely twisted together. It can be used as is, or the strands can be separated for use on a finer canvas.

You can also use tapestry yarn on No. 10 mono mesh. Slightly thinner than Persian, but just as strong, tapestry yarn consists of only one strand which cannot be separated.

When working on No. 12 mono mesh (with smaller holes), use two strands of Persian yarn or use tapestry yarn.

Both types of yarn can be bought at crafts, sewing, or department stores.

You will need about 1⅓ yards of yarn to cover each square inch (a hundred stitches) of No. 10 canvas. So choose your yarn carefully. Some brands aren't as good as others and will separate when you work. If you are planning to try a brand you haven't used before, it is best not to buy large quantities until you have stitched a small swatch to make sure the yarn will cover your canvas completely.

THIMBLE AND SCISSORS

You should use a plastic or metal thimble on the middle finger of the hand with which you sew. Although some people feel a thimble is unnecessary, doing needlepoint without one can be painful and cause callouses.

Scissors should be small and sharp for cutting yarn and removing mistakes. If you are going to put together your own needlepoint bag so you can stitch on the move, it's probably better to invest in a pair of folding scissors. They're safer and take up less room.

THE BASIC STITCHES

The basic needlepoint stitch is called the *tent stitch*. It always slants from the lower left to the upper right.

There are three ways to sew the tent stitch—in horizontal, vertical, or diagonal rows on the canvas. When stitching a single row, outlining a letter of your saying, or sewing a border, it is easier to work the tent stitch in vertical or horizontal rows across the canvas. This way, it is possible to create a thin line of color.

When the tent stitch is worked in horizontal or vertical rows, it is called the *continental stitch*.

For filling in larger areas, such as the background of your pillow or the inside of a letter, it's usually easier to work the tent stitch in diagonal rows.

When the tent stitch is worked in diagonal rows, it is called the *basket-weave stitch* because it creates a woven appearance on the back of the canvas.

Although you will probably use the basket-weave stitch most of the time, it's important to become familiar with the continental stitch as well, so you can switch directions as necessary to accommodate your design.

But remember that whether you use the continental or basket-weave stitch, all the stitches in your work should always look exactly the same, slanting from left to right, on the front side of the canvas.

THREADING THE NEEDLE

Threading the relatively thick needlepoint yarn can be frustrating unless you follow this method. Although it sounds a bit complicated, it only takes about a minute to learn and a few seconds to perform.

First cut a piece of yarn about 30 inches long. Then, holding the needle firmly in one hand, fold the yarn over with the other and make a small, tight loop of yarn around the eye. Next, slide this loop off the needle, still gripping the yarn together, and push it through the eye.

You are now ready to stitch.

THE CONTINENTAL STITCH

Do not knot the yarn. Instead, bring the needle up through the canvas, leaving a one-inch tail of yarn behind. Holding it gently in place with your finger, work your first stitches over this tail to secure it.

When you come to the end of your piece of yarn, no knot is necessary. Simply run your needle through some completed stitches on the back of your work and snip the needle free.

Working across the canvas in rows from right to left, follow fig. 1. Keep in mind that it's much easier to work if you complete each stitch in a single motion. For each stitch, you must go down through one hole and up through another. Pull the yarn through to complete the stitch only after your needle comes up on the front side of the canvas.

You should be holding the needle so that it is pointing diagonally while you stitch.

At the end of the row, simply turn your work upside down, and you're ready for the next row.

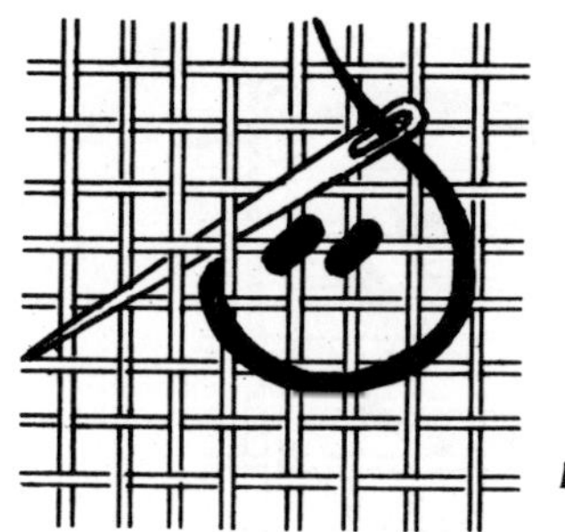
FIG. 1

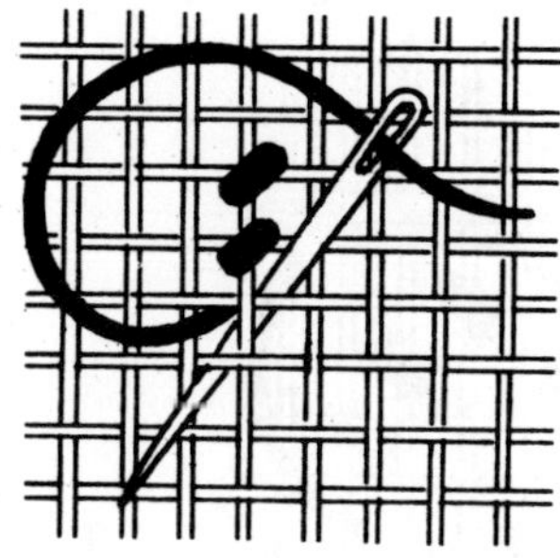
FIG. 2

To work the continental stitch vertically, from top to bottom, follow fig. 2. At the end of the row, turn the work upside down and go on to the next row. The needle should again be held in the diagonal position.

THE BASKET-WEAVE STITCH

The basket-weave stitch is the most fun to do, which is fortunate, since it's the one you will be using most of the time. This is the best stitch for covering large areas and getting out of tight spots such as corners.

The stitch is worked in interlocking diagonal rows, each longer than the last. But unlike working with the continental stitch, the canvas is never turned upside down when doing the basket weave. Each new row is stitched directly to the left of the previous row. The result, as you can see in fig. 12, is a growing triangular cluster of stitches.

Remember that it's important to complete each stitch in a single motion, pulling the yarn through completely on only the front side of the canvas.

If you're stitching the basket weave correctly, your needle will always point in a certain direction when you pick up the threads of the canvas to complete your stitch.

If you're stitching up a diagonal row, your needle should always be held horizontally and pointing to the left, as in fig. 3. If you're stitching down a diagonal row, your needle should be held vertically and pointing downward, as in fig. 4.

FIG. 3

FIG. 4

And when you sew the turning stitch at the beginning of each row in order to change direction, your needle should be held diagonally and to the left, as in fig. 8.

Leaving a one-inch tail of yarn on the back side of the canvas, follow fig. 5 to bring your yarn up through the canvas to begin your first stitch.

Following fig. 6, insert your needle down into the hole diagonally above and to the right. Next, bring your needle up through the canvas in the hole directly below the hole in which you began. Pull the yarn through gently, and you have just completed a stitch.

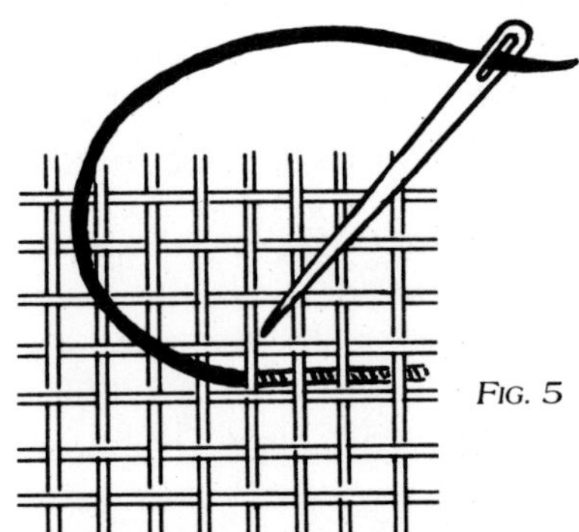

FIG. 5

FIG. 6

To continue, follow fig. 7, placing your next stitch directly beneath the first. Your needle is now in place for stitch number three.

Following fig. 8, place your third stitch directly to the left of your first stitch. Your needle is now in place for stitch number four, the first stitch of the next row.

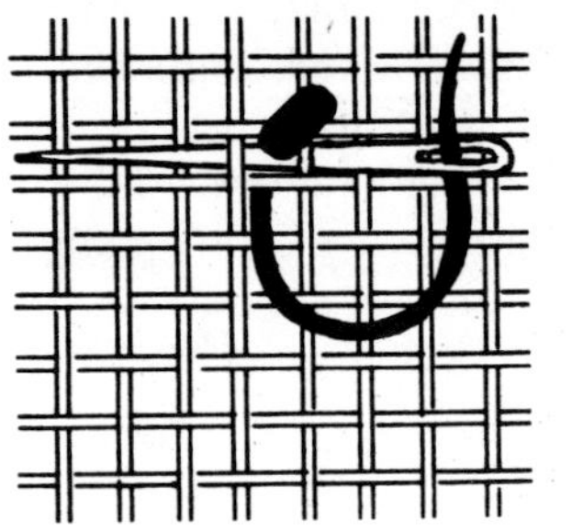

FIG. 7

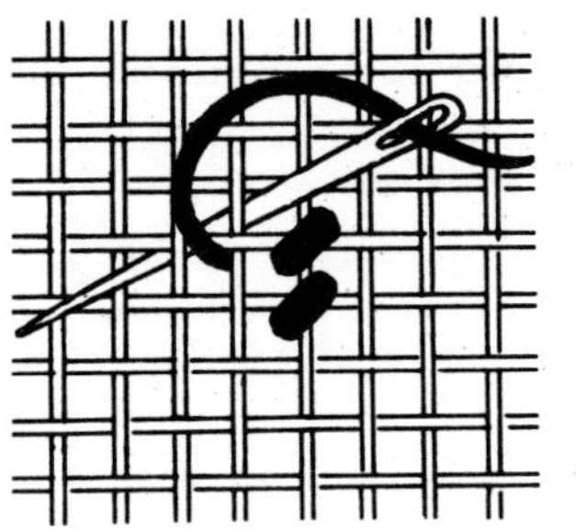

FIG. 8

Fig. 9 shows how to complete your fourth stitch, and sets you up for the fifth. Following figs. 10 and 11, continue stitching down the diagonal in the same pattern.

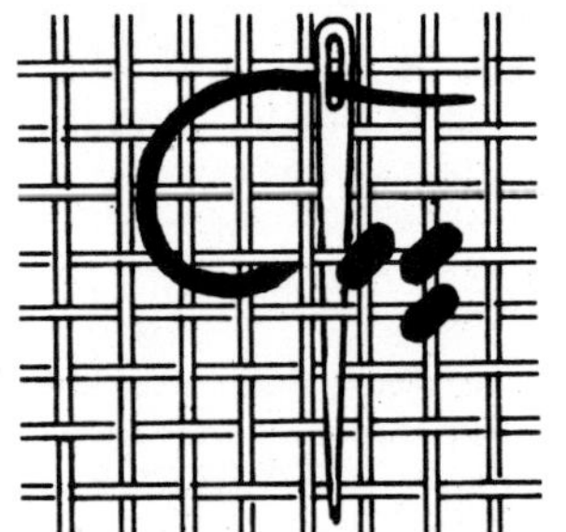

FIG. 9

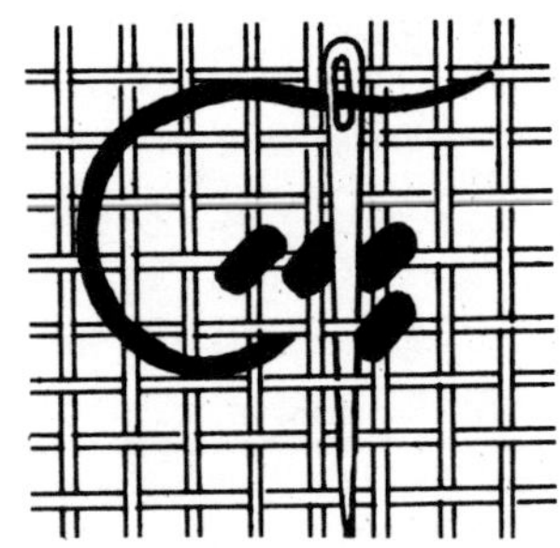

FIG. 10

Again, when you come to the end of that row, follow fig. 11 and place a turning stitch directly underneath your last stitch. This turning stitch is the first stitch of your new row, as in fig. 12.

The idea is to use the basket-weave stitch to work your way out of a corner with longer and longer diagonal rows. When stitching most of the background, all rows going up the diagonal should end

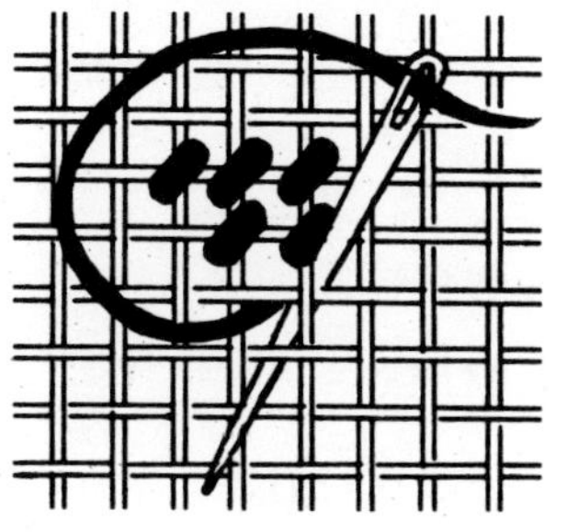

FIG. 11

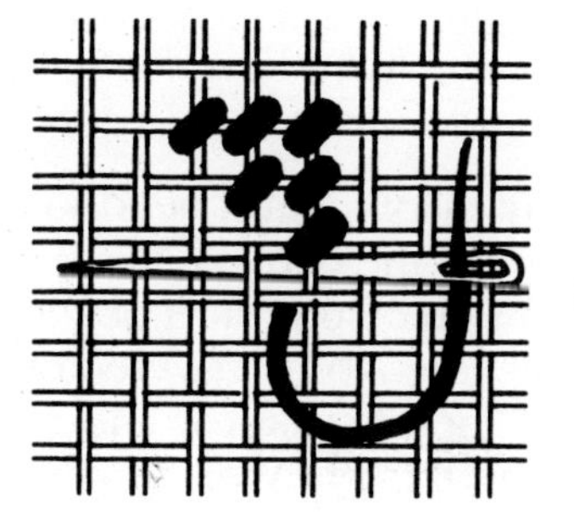

FIG. 12

at the same top point, forming a straight horizontal line along the top. All rows going down the diagonal should end along a straight line to the left or right, resulting in a growing triangular cluster of stitches. When working inside or around the letters, however, place your turning stitches to fit the shape you are trying to fill.

Remember, each row should be stitched in the *opposite* direction of the row last completed. Two adjacent rows worked in the same direction will create a line on the front of your work.

If you forget the direction in which you stitched your last row, simply turn the canvas over. If the last row of stitches on the back points horizontally, you last stitched up the canvas. If it points vertically, you last stitched down the canvas.

STITCHING TIPS

Yarn has its own tension. If you stitch too tightly, it will thin out and not cover the canvas completely. Since your stitches aren't meant to hold anything together, stitch gently, allowing the yarn to rest on the canvas and find its own tension.

No matter how gently you stitch, however, the yarn will become twisted as you work. When this happens, hold the canvas up and let the yarn fall freely. It will unwind itself.

HOW TO CORRECT A MISTAKE

Once you've learned the basic stitches, you'll find that needlepoint has a rhythm so relaxing that it can be done almost automatically. But don't let it become too automatic, lest you end up stitching where you hadn't intended to.

If you do make a mistake, it's easy to remove your wandering stitches with a little patience and some small, sharp scissors. Do not try to retrace the steps your needle took. Instead, working on the front side of your canvas, gently lift the stitches one at a time with the point of your scissors and snip them in half.

Any mistake can be corrected, as long as you're careful not to cut the canvas. Remember not to knot the remaining loose ends, but to reweave them through other stitches on the back side of the canvas.

BEFORE YOU BEGIN

After you've chosen a saying to stitch—but before you buy even an inch of mono mesh—you must determine how much canvas you will need to complete your project.

In each diagram, one box equals one stitch, and ten stitches equal one inch, on No. 10 mono mesh canvas. If you are using No. 12 canvas, twelve stitches equal one inch; on No. 14 canvas, there are fourteen stitches to one inch, and so on.

Remember that the larger the number of the mono mesh, the smaller your design will be—and vice versa. A design stitched on No. 5 mono mesh will be twice as large as the same design stitched on No. 10 mono mesh.

So, in order to figure out how much canvas you will need, follow this simple formula: saying + background + border + extra canvas needed for blocking = total amount of canvas needed.

If you're not good with numbers, don't panic. Adding up all the elements by this method is easy; it takes longer to explain than to do.

To figure out how many boxes your saying will take up, count the boxes in the diagram, from the first to last letter on the longest horizontal line of the saying. Then count the number of boxes that your saying takes up vertically. (Don't count extra height added by apostrophes.) For example, the saying "HA!" on page 34 fills up 78 boxes horizontally and 40 boxes vertically.

Then add 5 boxes on each side and 15 boxes at both top and bottom to allow space for sufficient background. (If your saying is taller than it is wide, you may have to reverse this rule, adding 15 boxes to each side and 5 to both the top and the bottom to balance it.)

"HA!" now takes up 88 boxes horizontally and 70 boxes vertically.

Next, choose one of the borders on pages 137–40. Then add the number of boxes the border contains to each side of the work. For example, if you decide to use border A, my favorite, which looks good on any pillow, you'll need to add another 10 boxes to each of the four sides of the canvas.

"HA!" now measures 108 boxes horizontally and 90 boxes vertically, the total area to be covered by needlepoint.

You will need to know the measurements of your design in inches. To get this number, simply divide the number of boxes horizontally and vertically by the gauge number of the mono mesh you are using. For example, if you are using No. 10 mono mesh, divide the number of boxes horizontally and vertically by 10. Using that formula, "HA!" measures 10.8 inches by 9 inches. You can round off 10.8 inches to 11 inches to make it easier. If you are using No. 12 mono mesh, "HA!" will measure about 9 inches by 7½ inches.

Measure the design that you have chosen in the same way and note down the results.

Finally, beyond the area taken up by your saying, the background, and the border, you need to have at least 1½ inches of extra canvas on each side to be used later for blocking and finishing your needlepoint.

Therefore, if you were to choose to stitch the saying "HA!" you would need a piece of No. 10 mono mesh canvas measuring a total of at least 14 inches by 12 inches. If you were using No. 12 mono mesh, you would need a piece that measured at least 12 inches by 10½ inches.

Once you have measured your canvas, cut it down to the correct size and fold a one-inch-wide piece of masking tape in half over each edge to prevent unraveling.

One edge of your canvas may already have been bound together by the manufacturer. This prefinished edge is called the selvage. If your canvas has a selvage, hold it to the left when transferring your design and when stitching your needlepoint.

The next step is to find the center of the canvas and mark it lightly with a permanent marker. This is essential in transferring your saying onto the canvas correctly.

Finding the center of any piece of canvas is easy. Simply fold the canvas in half and then in half again, and mark the center point where all the folds converge.

You are now ready to paint your saying onto the canvas and begin stitching.

TRANSFERRING YOUR SAYING TO THE CANVAS

As a needlework designer in a shop on New York's Madison Avenue, I designed and painted patterns on needlepoint canvases and matched them with brightly colored yarns. The shop sold these custom-made kits for fifty to two hundred dollars.

Although the patterns in this book can be stitched directly from the diagrams, you can make your own needlepoint kits by painting your chosen pattern directly onto the canvas. Add yarn and needles to complete it, and your custom-made needlepoint kit is ready to stitch or be given to a needlepoint-loving friend in a colorful basket or bag. Best of all, the kit costs you only what you spent for the materials.

In order to transfer a saying onto the canvas correctly, you will need to find the center point of that saying as it is charted on the diagram in this book.

You can find the center by counting the number of boxes both horizontally and vertically and dividing each number by two.

It is important to keep a few things in mind when counting boxes on the saying diagram. The sayings in this book were charted on graph paper and centered on the page, and that is how they appear in the saying diagrams. To make counting easier, every fifth box is marked by a heavier line.

When transferring your saying onto the canvas, remember this simple rule: one box in the saying diagram = one stitch = one intersection of threads on the canvas.

The center of a saying remains the same no matter what size the border or background used. If a saying takes up an odd number of boxes horizontally, its center will fall on a thread of the canvas. If a saying takes up an even number of boxes horizontally, its center will fall between two threads of the canvas.

But wherever it falls, you will be using the center as a reference point when transferring. Therefore, it is important that you locate it correctly and that you are able to match up the center of your canvas with the center of your saying.

If you have not matched the centers, you may find that after transferring half of your design onto the mesh, you don't have enough room for the rest of it.

And remember that the center of your saying remains the same no matter what size background or border you add.

On the diagrams in this book, the letters of the sayings are shaded in gray. The backgrounds are unshaded. If the letters of a saying have stitched outlines around them, this is indicated with a heavy black line one box wide. Some letters also have "shadows," which should be marked on the canvas and stitched in a color that contrasts with the letters themselves.

To transfer a letter to the canvas, count the number of boxes that the letter takes up in each direction. Then count the corresponding number of threads on the canvas before you mark the canvas or begin stitching.

For example, when transferring a part of a letter 7 boxes high and 2 boxes wide, you must count seven threads up on the canvas and two threads over. That part of the letter will end up 7 stitches high and 2 stitches wide.

Simple letters, such as stick letters that are one box wide, are easiest to transfer to the canvas and stitch. More ornate letters that are thicker than one box wide or have stitched outlines or shading in another color are more difficult to both transfer and stitch. So beginners might want to practice transferring and stitching some simple letters first.

Transfer your design from the center of the canvas outward, using the center mark as a reference point. Use only a permanent marker to paint your saying on the mesh. A pen, pencil, or regular marker will come off on your hands and discolor the yarn while you stitch, and later, it will bleed when you block your finished work.

Even some markers that are made for fabric are not permanent enough. You can test a marker by coloring a small piece of mesh. Let it dry for fifteen minutes, and then run the mesh under warm water. If any of the color comes off, don't use the marker.

Generally, the less ink on the canvas, the better. So unless you're making your kit as a gift, it's best to color in only the letters and the border of the saying and leave the background white.

If you decide to color in the letters, border, and background, however, *paint the lighter-colored areas first.* For example, if you want green letters on a yellow background, go over the entire work area with yellow, let it dry, and then color the letters green. If the background is to be green, color the letters yellow first.

Use fine-line or bullet markers for outlining, and broad markers for large areas. Always use markers in colors that come as close as possible to the shades of yarn you're using.

Paint lightly with short, even strokes, covering each thread with a single stroke. If you press too hard, the color will spread onto adjacent threads.

If you make a mistake, don't panic. After all, you are simply making a map, and shortly your design will be covered by yarn. If you want to fix it, however, wait until the ink is dry. Then go over your mistake with white acrylic paint, using a thin paintbrush. Use the paint sparingly, for too thick a coat will crack. When the paint is dry, you can go over it with your marker.

COLOR SUGGESTIONS

Before you buy the yarn for your project, you should think carefully about color. A clever saying, beautifully stitched, will lose all its pizzazz without the right colors to back it up.

You must choose colors that not only are pretty, but are also in high contrast to one another. If the shades used for the letters and background are too similar, your saying will be hard to read and it will fail to create the visual excitement that is possible.

These pillows look best in lively brights and rich pastels. To help you choose from the rainbow of colors available, the color chart on page 21 lists 25 bright, pastel, and neutral colors which are my favorites for these projects. The chart lists the colors and the corresponding color numbers of two popular brands of yarn, Paternayan and D.M.C.

Mix and match as you choose—all the colors in the chart look great together. I find, however, that when I stitch a pillow with border A, for example, just three colors plus white works well. I use one color for the letters, one for the background, another for the border stripe next to the background, white for the middle stripe, and the letter color for the last stripe around the edge of the work.

I've also found that light letters against a dark background give the pillows a dramatic look. Some sayings have added drama built in with letters that are shaded. The shading does not have to be darker than the letters, however. Using a lighter color for shading can provide an interesting visual contrast.

Some "can't miss" color combinations for great gifts are: red letters, yellow background, blue border; green letters, pink background, red border; aqua letters, purple background, magenta border; yellow letters, purple background, pink border; and dark blue letters, light blue background, orange border. White letters always look great on a red, green, or blue background.

I have listed the colors that I like best, but it's you who will be making a pillow for someone you know, or to match the colors of a special room. Yarn comes in hundreds of colors to fit any personality or coordinate with any couch or easy chair where your pillow will eventually rest.

MY FAVORITE COLORS

COLOR	PATERNAYAN YARN NO.	D.M.C. YARN NO.
Red	941	7544
Cardinal Red	972	7606
Dark Blue	542	7797
Navy	571	7247
Emerald	684	7911
Golden Yellow	770	7436
Canary Yellow	772	7433
Magenta	352	7155
Aqua	583	7996
Fuchsia	353	7153
Hot Pink	962	7603
Violet	301	7708
Purple	331	7243
Orange	811	7947
Apple Green	632	7342
Pastel Pink	945	7133
Pastel Blue	584	7313
Mint	594	7604
Pale Yellow	762	7727
Lilac	304	7896
Peach	845	7853
Pearl Gray	203	7715
Gray	210	7713
Black	—	—
White	—	—

BORDERS

All the sayings in this book were diagrammed without borders, but no pillow should be without one as an elegant finishing touch.

You can choose from the four striped borders I've included on pages 137–40, or you can devise one of your own, with a different kind of stripe or another motif. But keep in mind that a simple border works best, enhancing rather than overpowering the letters.

All the borders are one inch wide on each side, and they coordinate with all the sayings in this book. I've found, however, that sayings with skinny letters generally look better with borders that have thin stripes, while sayings with wider letters look better with borders that have thicker stripes.

My favorite, border A, happens to look great with any saying.

WORKING TIPS

Stitch the letters of your saying before you stitch the background or the border. After finishing the letters, stitch the background from right to left and from top to bottom, always stitching toward the unworked portion of the canvas. This makes stitching easier, since your needle does not have to fight for space in a hole where a stitch has already been placed.

The canvas has been measured, the center marked, the saying transferred, the yarn chosen, and the stitches learned. Now your custom-made needlepoint kit is ready to travel with you anywhere, to be picked up at a moment's notice when you're bored, or to stay at home and relax with you in front of the fire.

FINISHING YOUR NEEDLEPOINT

The first thing you should do upon finishing your needlepoint is make sure that you haven't left out any stitches. You can check by holding your work in front of a window. If any bright dots of light show through, stitches are missing. If you have left any out, put them in before going any further.

You can make a pillow out of your needlepoint either by hand or on a sewing machine. If you plan to use a sewing machine, however, you will need to needlepoint two extra rows around the entire perimeter of your work . Use the same color yarn as the last row of the border of your design.

But before you make your needlepoint into anything, it should be washed if it's dirty, and it must be blocked.

Many people don't feel comfortable washing needlepoint, but I do. And if you wash it carefully, your needlepoint will look better and be easier to block. If you decide to wash your work, however, you must do it before blocking. Needlepoint will need reblocking each time it's washed.

To wash your needlepoint, treat it as you would any fine wool sweater. Use only a cold-water wool wash or a liquid soap for fine washables. Wet your work completely, but do not scrub or wring it. Let the dirt soak out. Then rinse gently and roll the needlepoint in a towel to remove excess water.

When your needlepoint is clean and still damp, it is a perfect time to block it.

BLOCKING YOUR WORK

Even if you have been extremely careful in handling your work, chances are that by the time you've finished, the canvas has been pulled out of its original square or rectangular shape. Blocking will square it once more.

Since these pieces are small, it is often possible to get them back into shape simply by ironing. Preheat your steam iron on the wool setting. With the front side of the work face down, pull your needlepoint in the opposite direction from which it is slanting and iron it, using steam, in that direction at the same time.

If your work is still out of shape after ironing, however, it will be necessary to block it. Your needlepoint must be damp in order to be blocked correctly. If you decide not to wash it first, spray it lightly with water using a plant sprayer.

Blocking your work won't take much effort or equipment. All you need is a two-foot-square piece of homosote board from your local lumberyard, some brown wrapping paper, a ruler, and rustproof pushpins or a staple gun. Do not use plywood for blocking as it's too hard a material for this purpose.

In order to get your work back into shape, you need to know its original shape and dimensions. When you first figured out how much canvas you would need for your pillow, you should have noted down the dimensions in inches of the total area covered by needlepoint. If you didn't, do it now, using the method described starting on page 18.

Using a ruler, measure a rectangle (or square) of the same dimensions on the wrapping paper and cut it out carefully. Your goal is to pull the slanting sides of your work back into shape so that they line up with the straight sides of the paper rectangle.

The first step is to securely tape the rectangle down on the homosote board and place your needlepoint face down on top of it. Then spray the back of your needlepoint lightly with water until damp and pull it gently in the opposite direction from which it is slanting. Continue tugging, gently but firmly, until all the corners line up with the corners of the paper rectangle.

When all the corners and the sides line up perfectly, push a pin (or put a staple) through the mesh and into the board in the center of each side, about half an inch away from the last row of stitches. Continue adding pins or staples along each side, half an inch apart, until all sides and the corners have been pinned to the board. Spray again.

The next step is easy—leave your needlepoint on the board for at least twenty-four hours to dry.

To remove your work from the board, use a screwdriver to gently pry up staples or stubborn pushpins. If the needlepoint is still out of shape, however, don't reblock it. Instead, follow the instructions given above for ironing, and your needlepoint should finally regain its original shape.

After you have completed the blocking process, trim off all excess canvas and tape to half an inch all around and spread a thin line of white glue over all edges to prevent unraveling. You can accomplish the same thing by machine-stitching over the edges.

TURNING YOUR NEEDLEPOINT INTO A PILLOW

Since you've come this far, don't shy away from this last leg of your project. Making your needlepoint into a magnificent pillow is easy—even if you've never sewn anything before.

So, put aside your needlepoint for the half hour it will take you to make the inner pillow upon which your needlepoint "pillowcase" will rest.

THE INNER PILLOW

The inner pillow is made of plain muslin, which is sold by the yard at fabric stores. You should buy enough so that you can cut two pieces which each measure two inches wider and two inches longer than your needlepoint.

For example, if your needlepoint measures 14 inches by 16 inches, you should buy a piece of muslin that measures at least 16 inches by 36 inches and cut it into two pieces that each measure 16 inches by 18 inches.

After it's sewn, your inner pillow should measure one inch longer and wider than your needlepoint.

Put the two pieces together, line up the edges, and sew a seam half an inch from the edge on three of the sides, by hand or with a sewing machine.

Next, turn the pillow inside out and fill it with Dacron pillow stuffing, available at fabric, craft, and department stores. Coax the stuffing into the corners with a crochet hook, a knitting needle, or the eraser end of a pencil. Be careful not to overstuff. Your pillow should be firm and gently rounded, not a hard lump.

Lastly, sew up the fourth side.

CHOOSING A BACKING

Your muslin inner pillow will go inside a "pillowcase" made up of your needlepoint on one side and a fabric backing on the other. You can sew the two together either by hand or with a sewing machine, but you should know in advance which method you are going to use so you can choose a suitable fabric for the backing.

If you are going to sew your pillow together by hand, choose a loosely woven fabric or a felt through which a large needle and yarn can pass easily.

If you are going to use a sewing machine, you can choose almost any fabric, such as a velvet or even a wool, that matches the couch or easy chair where your pillow will eventually rest.

In addition, remember that if you are going to finish your pillow on a sewing machine, you will need to have stitched an extra two rows of needlepoint on each side. (See page 22.)

Whether you sew your pillow by hand or machine, the material should be the size of the total area covered by needlepoint plus half an inch on each side for seam allowance.

FINISHING YOUR PILLOW BY HAND

At this point, you should have about half an inch of unstitched mesh on each of the four sides of your needlepoint. If you have more than that, trim it now, being careful not to overdo it.

Next, with the back side of the canvas facing you, fold each corner over half an inch and then cut off the corner diagonally to a quarter of an inch. Using steam, press with an iron on the wool setting. Then fold over the half-inch margins of mesh on the sides, one at a time, leaving two lines of mesh showing at each of the edges. Press in place.

Fold and press your backing material in the same manner, folding over only half an inch on each side. Do this even if you are using felt, which does not unravel.

Your needlepoint and backing should now be the same size.

SELF-CORDING YOUR PILLOW

By sewing your pillow together by hand, you will make it look even prettier with this extremely simple, yet decorative, self-cording stitch. It is called self-cording because the double strand of yarn used gives the edges of the pillow a thick, corded effect.

Back sides together, line up the edges of your needlepoint and backing and pin them in place. Thread your needle with a 60-inch piece of yarn in a coordinating or contrasting color. Then perform this little trick and your yarn will remain even and glide more smoothly through the canvas and backing.

Pull the strand of yarn through the needle's eye so that the needle is in the middle. Then stitch through the two strands, as close to the needle's eye as possible, and pull the yarn straight.

Hold your work with the backing of the needlepoint toward you and the edge up, rather than flat in your lap. You will be stitching from right to left.

To begin, draw your needle through a few stitches on the back side of the canvas near the upper right corner. As usual, leave a small tail of yarn, but do not make a knot.

Beginning at the right corner, bring your needle through the backing and insert it into the first hole of the empty row of mesh showing at the edge of the work. Pull the yarn gently, but firmly, and insert your needle into the backing again and into the next box of mesh on the left. Pull the yarn through once more, and you have just completed your first stitch.

Although your needlepoint stitches always slant from left to right, the self-cording stitch goes straight up and down, making a small loop of yarn over the edge of the pillow.

Work your stitches gently, being careful to keep all the loops approximately the same size, and you'll get a nice, even roll at the edge of your needlepoint.

When you reach a corner, turn the canvas so that the next side points upward. Two stitches in the corner hole should cover all the mesh. If not, don't keep adding stitches. Instead, use a waterproof marker the same color as the yarn to color any mesh that shows.

After stitching three sides of your pillow, insert your muslin inner pillow, using a crochet hook, a knitting needle, or the eraser end of a pencil to coax the pillow into the corners. Then finish the fourth side and end the yarn by slipping your needle through several stitches and cutting off the extra yarn. You'll find that if you pull gently on the corners of your pillow, the little tail of yarn will disappear.

FINISHING YOUR PILLOW BY MACHINE

When finishing your pillow by sewing machine, you can choose almost any fabric as a backing, although I don't recommend cotton, which is usually too delicate to stand up to long wear.

You will need a piece of fabric that is one inch wider and one inch longer than your needlepoint.

Remember that in order to finish your pillow by machine, you should have stitched two extra rows of needlepoint around all four sides of the canvas in the same color as the last row of your border. Take the measurements for your backing fabric only after those rows have been added.

With front sides facing, pin three sides of the fabric and needlepoint together. Using a sewing machine (you might need a thicker-than-normal needle), sew a seam half an inch from the edge of the backing and along the straight line in between the two rows of needlepoint. Go slowly, since sewing a straight line will greatly affect the look of your pillow.

After three sides have been sewn, cut each of the corners diagonally to a quarter of an inch beyond the extra rows of needlepoint. Turn your "pillowcase" inside out and press it in place.

Insert the muslin inner pillow, easing it into the corners with the end of a crochet hook, a knitting needle, or the eraser end of a pencil.

Then sew the fourth side closed by hand with sewing thread (not yarn), sewing into the last row of needlepoint stitches.

MAKING A DOOR SIGN

You can make a door sign out of a pillow by simply knotting the ends of a length of decorative rope or cord and inserting each end about half an inch from the corners on the top edge of the pillow. Sew the seam on that side around the cord.

FRAMING YOUR NEEDLEPOINT

To frame your needlepoint, trim the excess canvas along the edges to one inch on each side. Cut a piece of thin cardboard the same size as the total area covered by needlepoint and stretch your blocked needlepoint over the cardboard. Then fasten it on the back with strong fabric tape and slip it into a plastic box frame.

You can mount your work on a coordinating piece of fabric or colored paper. To do this, glue your needlepoint onto the fabric or paper and let it dry completely before finally slipping your masterpiece into the frame.

METRIC CONVERSION

You may wish to convert the measurements in this book, which are given in inches, to centimeters.

1 inch is approximately 2.5 centimeters
1 foot is approximately 3 decimeters
1 yard is approximately .9 meter

LIST OF DESIGNS

33 THINGS TODAY
ARE MORE
LIKE THEY'VE
EVER BEEN

34 HA!

35 THOSE WHO CAN, DO.
THOSE WHO CAN'T, TEACH.
THOSE WHO CAN'T TEACH,
TEACH GYM.

36 IF YOU
LAUGH A LOT
YOUR WRINKLES
WILL BE IN THE
RIGHT PLACES

37 TE AMO

38 SIXTY
IS
SEXY

39 A PERSON'S
NOSE AND EARS
CONTINUE TO GROW
THROUGHOUT
HIS OR HER
LIFETIME

40 ADAM: DO YOU
LOVE ME?
EVE: WHO ELSE?

41 WHEN IT'S ALL
SAID AND DONE
THERE'S NOTHING LEFT
TO SAY OR DO

42 THE BEST THINGS
IN LIFE
AREN'T THINGS

43 REAL MEN
DON'T HAVE
FLOPPY DISKS

44 IT WAS
SO COLD
I ALMOST
GOT MARRIED

45 THIS IS NO
DRESS REHEARSAL—
THIS IS IT

46 HE WHO
LAUGHS
LASTS

47 ONCE
I THOUGHT
I WAS WRONG—
BUT I WAS
MISTAKEN

48 NO PROBLEM
IS SO BIG
OR SO COMPLICATED
THAT IT CAN'T BE
RUN AWAY FROM

49 YOU'VE GOT
A LOT OF
CHUTZPAH

50 I'M THE
MOMMY,
THAT'S WHY

51 ANYONE WHO SAYS
MONEY CAN'T
BUY HAPPINESS
DOESN'T KNOW
WHERE TO SHOP

52 THE OLDER
THE VIOLIN
THE SWEETER
THE MUSIC

53 INCLUDE
ME OUT

54 THE
GODDESS
SLEEPS HERE

55 MOTHER
KNOWS
BEST

56 A FOOL
AND HIS MONEY
ARE SOON
INVITED
EVERYWHERE

57 MY MIND'S MADE UP
DON'T CONFUSE ME
WITH THE FACTS

58 I DON'T HAVE
STRESS
BUT I THINK
I MIGHT BE
A CARRIER

59 GO FOR IT

60 WHEN MY SHIP
COMES IN
I'LL PROBABLY
BE WAITING
AT THE AIRPORT

61 MY MAMMA
DIDN'T RAISE
NO FOOL

62 TO ERR IS
HUMAN,
BUT ISN'T IT
DIVINE?

63 I'M NOT
REALLY HEAVY—
I'M JUST
TOO SHORT

64 INFALLIBLE
BUT NOT
INFLEXIBLE

65 THE BEST MAN
FOR THE JOB
IS A WOMAN

66 I LOVE
CATS

67 GOD GRANT ME
THE SERENITY TO ACCEPT
THE THINGS I
CANNOT CHANGE,
COURAGE TO CHANGE
THE THINGS I CAN,
AND WISDOM TO KNOW
THE DIFFERENCE.

68 NONE
FOR THE
ROAD

69 ANY MAN CAN BE
A FATHER,
BUT IT TAKES
SOMEONE SPECIAL
TO BE A DADDY

70 IT AIN'T
OVER
TILL IT'S
OVER

71 DRESS BRITISH
THINK YIDDISH

72 STOP TALKING
WHILE I'M
INTERRUPTING

73 YOU HAVE TO KISS
A LOT OF TOADS
BEFORE YOU FIND A
HANDSOME PRINCE

74 A HYPOCHONDRIAC
IS SOMEONE WHO
CAN'T LEAVE BEING
WELL ENOUGH ALONE

75 DO IT,
DELEGATE IT,
OR DITCH IT.

76 I AM EASILY
SATISFIED
WITH THE
VERY BEST

77 LOVE ME
LOVE MY
DOG

78 GREAT MUSICIANS
NEVER DIE,
THEY JUST GO
FROM BAR TO BAR

79 HOMEWORK
GIVES ME
A RASH

80 IS THIS
DEAL
KOSHER?

81 IF YOU CAN'T
DAZZLE THEM
WITH BRILLIANCE
BAFFLE THEM
WITH BULLSHIT

82 YOU CAN
OBSERVE A LOT
JUST BY
WATCHING

83 IN REAL LIFE
THERE IS NO
ALGEBRA

84 THERE'S
ALWAYS ROOM
AT THE TOP

85 AUNTIE EM,
HATE YOU—
HATE KANSAS—
TAKING THE DOG.
DOROTHY

86 TO ERR IS HUMAN—
TO FORGIVE IS NOT
COMPANY POLICY

87 I LOVE
CHAMPAGNE
CAVIAR AND
CASH

88 GOD LOVES
WOMEN WITH
FAT THIGHS

89 IF YOU HAVEN'T
GOT ANYTHING
NICE TO SAY
ABOUT ANYBODY,
COME SIT
NEXT TO ME

90 I'M LITTLE
BUT PROGRAMMED
FOR BIG THINGS

91 MONEY ISN'T
EVERYTHING
BUT IT SURE
KEEPS THE KIDS
IN TOUCH

92 IT'S HARD
TO BE HUMBLE
WHEN YOU'RE AS
GREAT AS I AM

93 BUY
SHEEP
SELL
DEER

94 IF YOU
MUST SMOKE,
PLEASE DON'T
EXHALE

95 DON'T BLOW IT—
GOOD PLANETS
ARE HARD
TO FIND

96 I'M A LIBERATED
WOMAN—
I HAD SEX
BEFORE MARRIAGE
AND A JOB AFTER

97 ENJOY
YOURSELF—
IT'S LATER ON
YOU'LL THINK

98 DO YOUR
CHILDREN
KNOW WHERE
YOU ARE?

99 A DAY WITHOUT
SUNSHINE IS . . .
LIKE NIGHT

100 NO
NUKES

101 HOW BEAUTIFUL
IT IS TO DO
NOTHING
AND THEN REST
AFTERWARD

102 NON FUMARE
PER FAVORE

103 TOTO . . .
I HAVE A FEELING
WE'RE NOT IN
KANSAS ANYMORE

104 INSANITY
IS HEREDITARY.
YOU CAN GET IT
FROM YOUR
CHILDREN

105 TOO MUCH OF
A GOOD THING
IS WONDERFUL

106 FOR BETTER
FOR WORSE
BUT NOT
FOR LUNCH

107 A MAN
IS KNOWN BY
THE COMPANY
HE ORGANIZES

108 MY GET UP
AND GO
HAS GOT UP
AND GONE

109 THANK YOU
FOR NOT
WHIMPERING

110 YOU'RE
24
KARAT

111 YOU'LL NEVER
KNOW HOW MANY
FRIENDS YOU HAVE
TILL YOU GET
A SUMMER PLACE

112 I WATCH THE
PHIL DONAHUE
SHOW

113 IF YOU
LIVED HERE
YOU'D BE
HOME
BY NOW

114 BE
REASONABLE,
DO IT
MY WAY

115 WE'RE LIVING
HAPPILY
EVER AFTER
ON A DAY-TO-DAY
BASIS

116 MORAL
VICTORIES
DON'T COUNT

117 THE BEST
THINGS IN LIFE
ARE CHOCOLATE

118 HAPPINESS IS
POSITIVE
CASH FLOW

119 THERE'S
SOMETHING
ABOUT ME
I REALLY LIKE

120 LOVE
THY NEIGHBOR
BUT DON'T
GET CAUGHT

121 WHEN THE GOING
GETS TOUGH
THE TOUGH
GO SHOPPING

122 MY SON
IS
PERFECT

123 NINE OUT OF TEN
DOCTORS WHO
PREFERRED CAMELS
HAVE SWITCHED
BACK TO WOMEN

124 DID
SOMEBODY
MENTION
LUNCH?

125 I'VE TRIED
RELAXING
BUT I FEEL
MORE
COMFORTABLE
TENSE

126 LIVING WELL
IS THE BEST
REVENGE

127 ONCE
YOU'RE OVER
THE HILL
YOU PICK UP
SPEED

128 ALL YOU
ROCK PEOPLE
DOWN
AT THE ROXY
AND UP
IN THE ROCKIES
ROCK ON

129 WHEN I WANT
YOUR OPINION
I'LL GIVE IT TO YOU

130 MY OTHER
HOME IS
IMMACULATE

131 I'D LIKE TO BECOME
AN OPTIMIST
BUT I DOUBT IF
IT WOULD WORK OUT

132 AGE ONLY
MATTERS
IF YOU ARE
A WINE

133 I'M ALWAYS
THERE WHEN
I NEED YOU

137 BORDER A

138 BORDER B

139 BORDER C

140 BORDER D

THE DESIGN DIAGRAMS

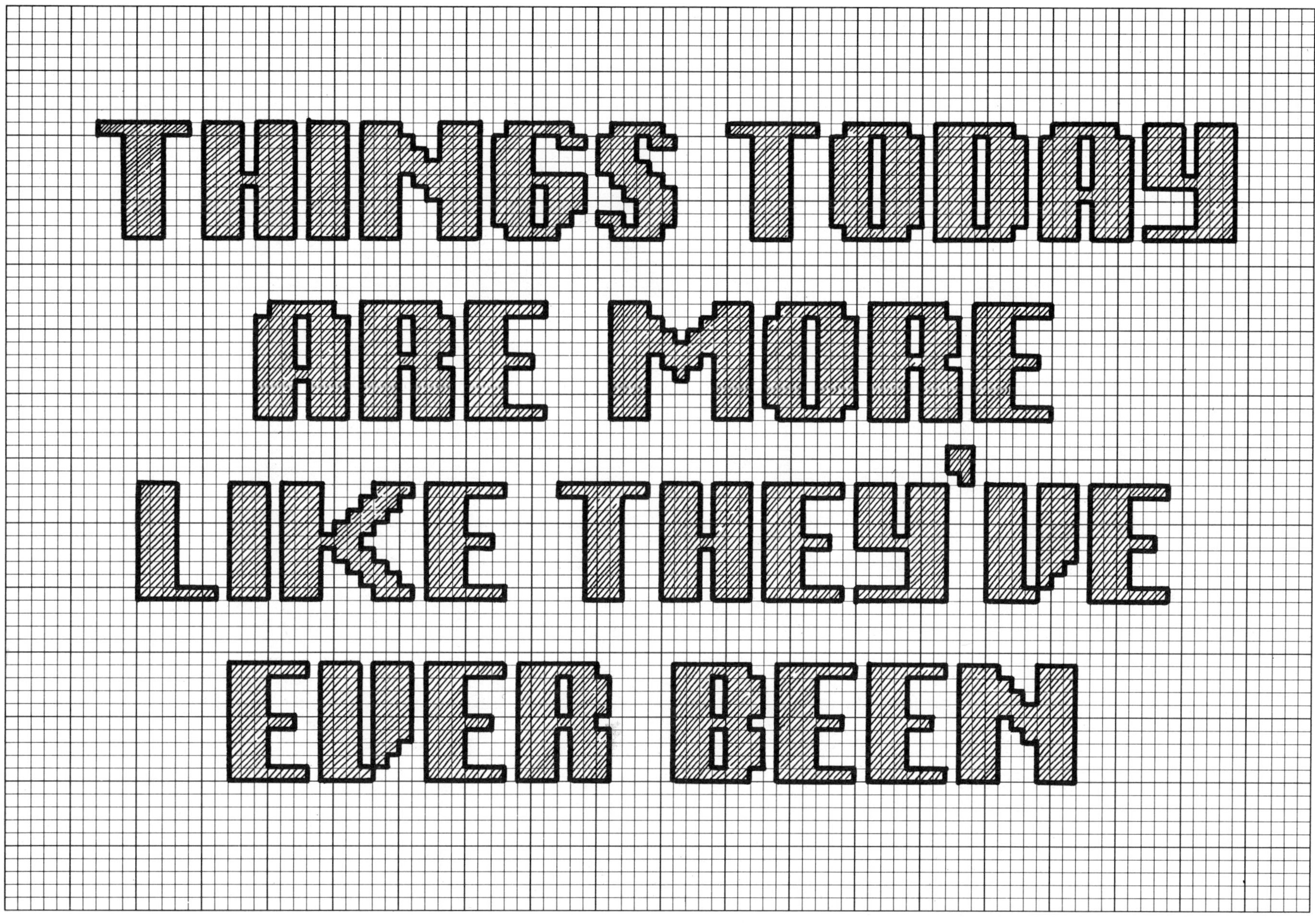
THINGS TODAY
ARE MORE
LIKE THEY'VE
EVER BEEN

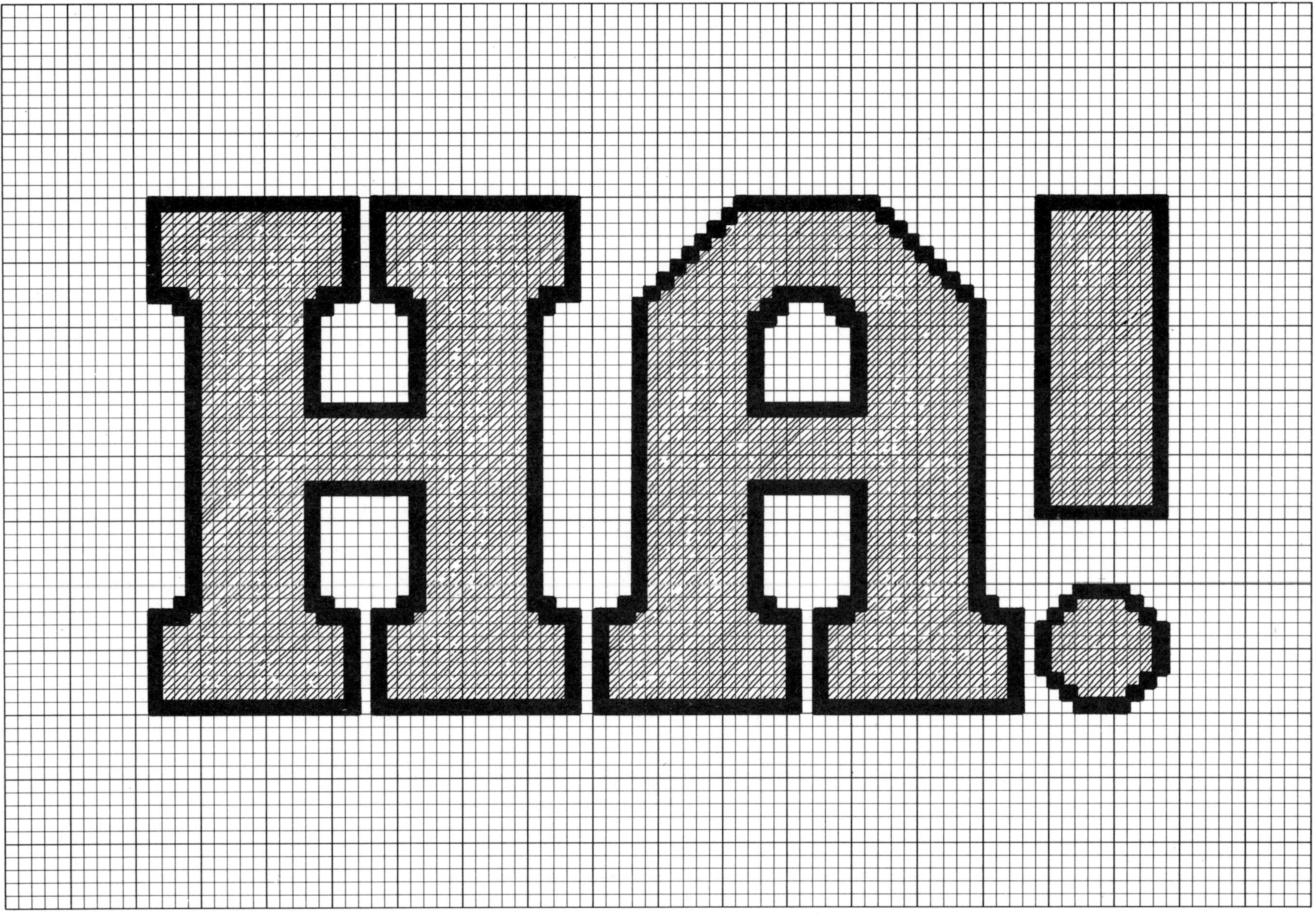
HA!

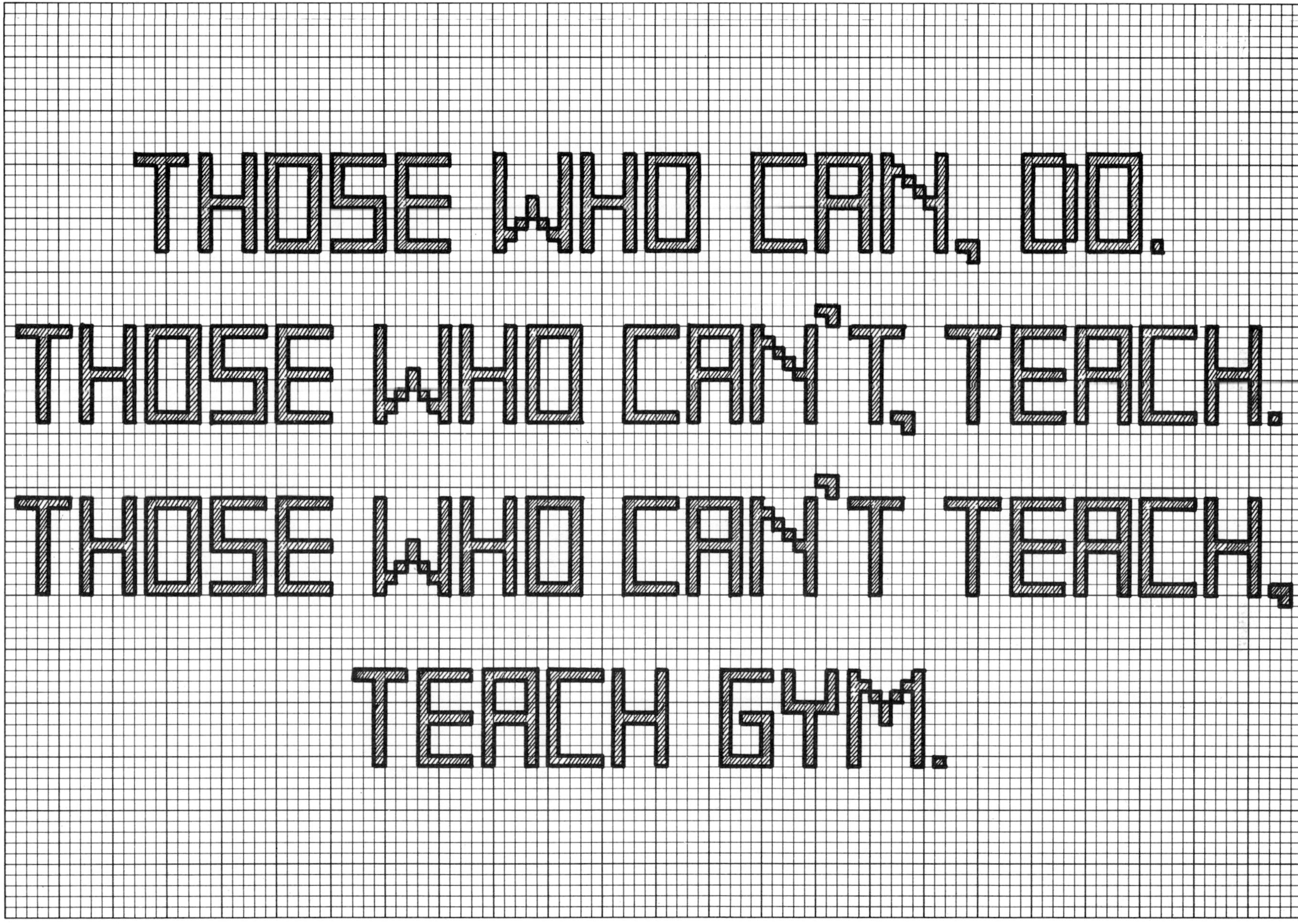
THOSE WHO CAN, DO.
THOSE WHO CAN'T, TEACH.
THOSE WHO CAN'T TEACH,
TEACH GYM.

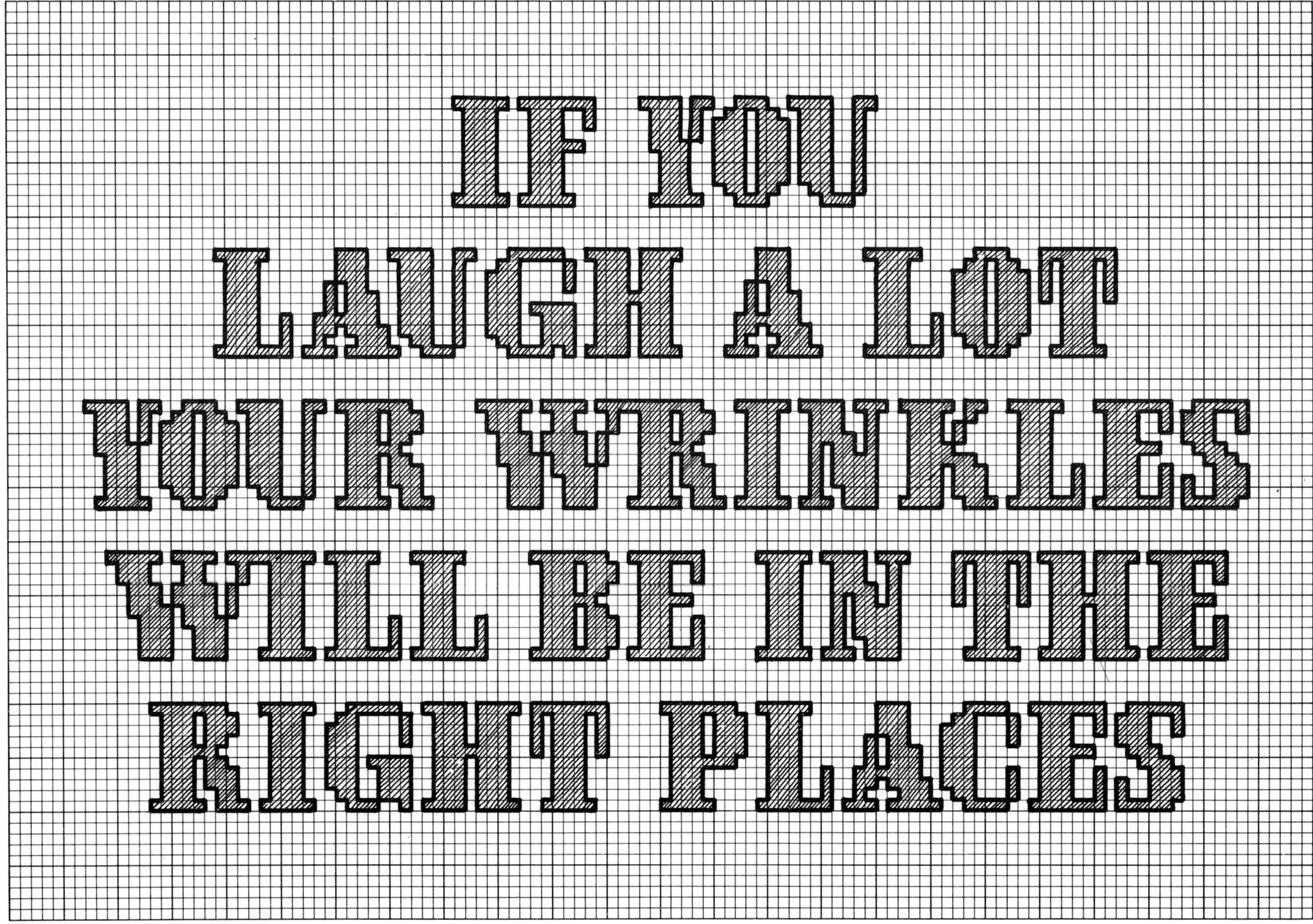
IF YOU
LAUGH A LOT
YOUR WRINKLES
WILL BE IN THE
RIGHT PLACES

TE AMO

SIXTY
IS
SEXY

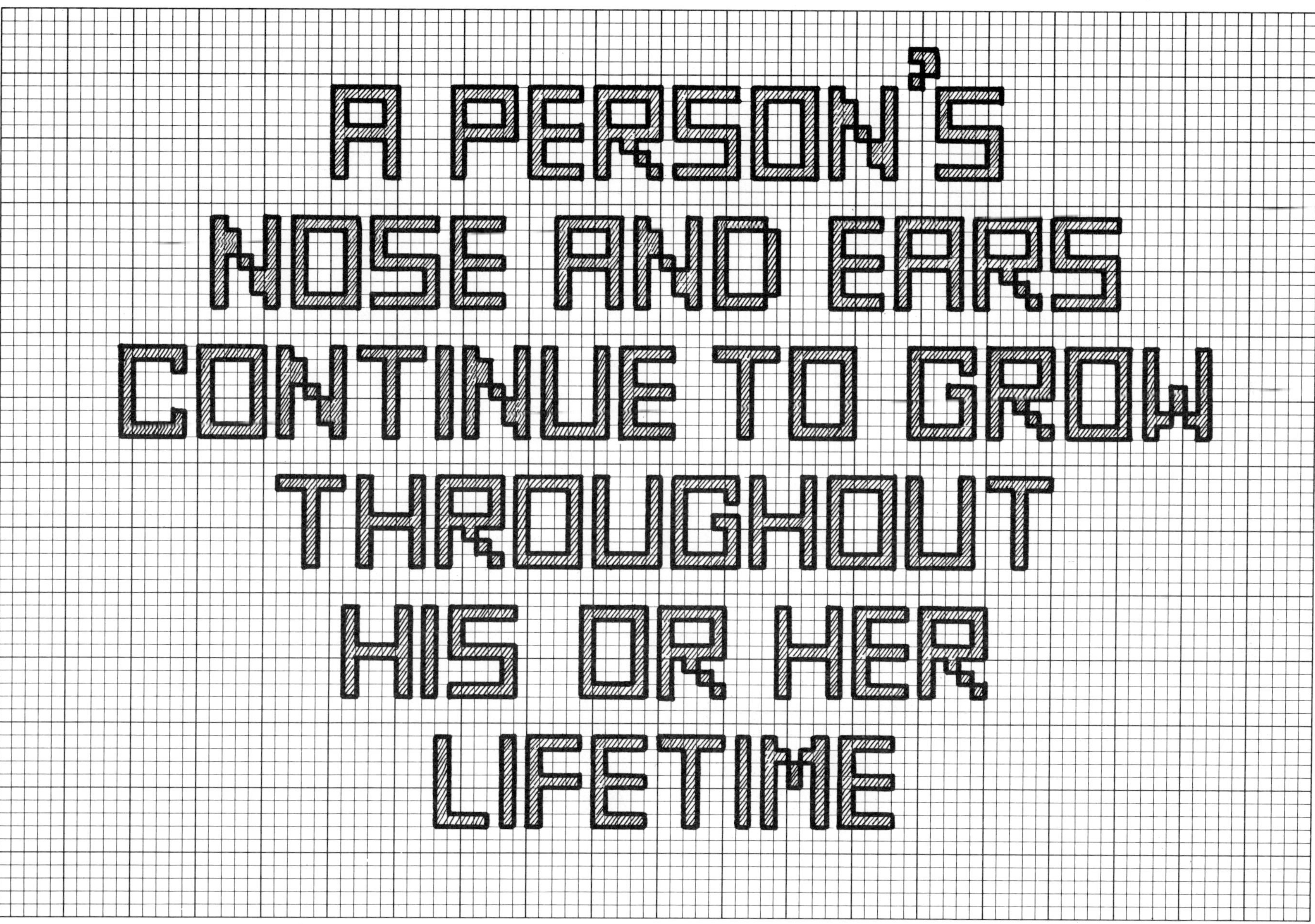
A PERSON'S
NOSE AND EARS
CONTINUE TO GROW
THROUGHOUT
HIS OR HER
LIFETIME

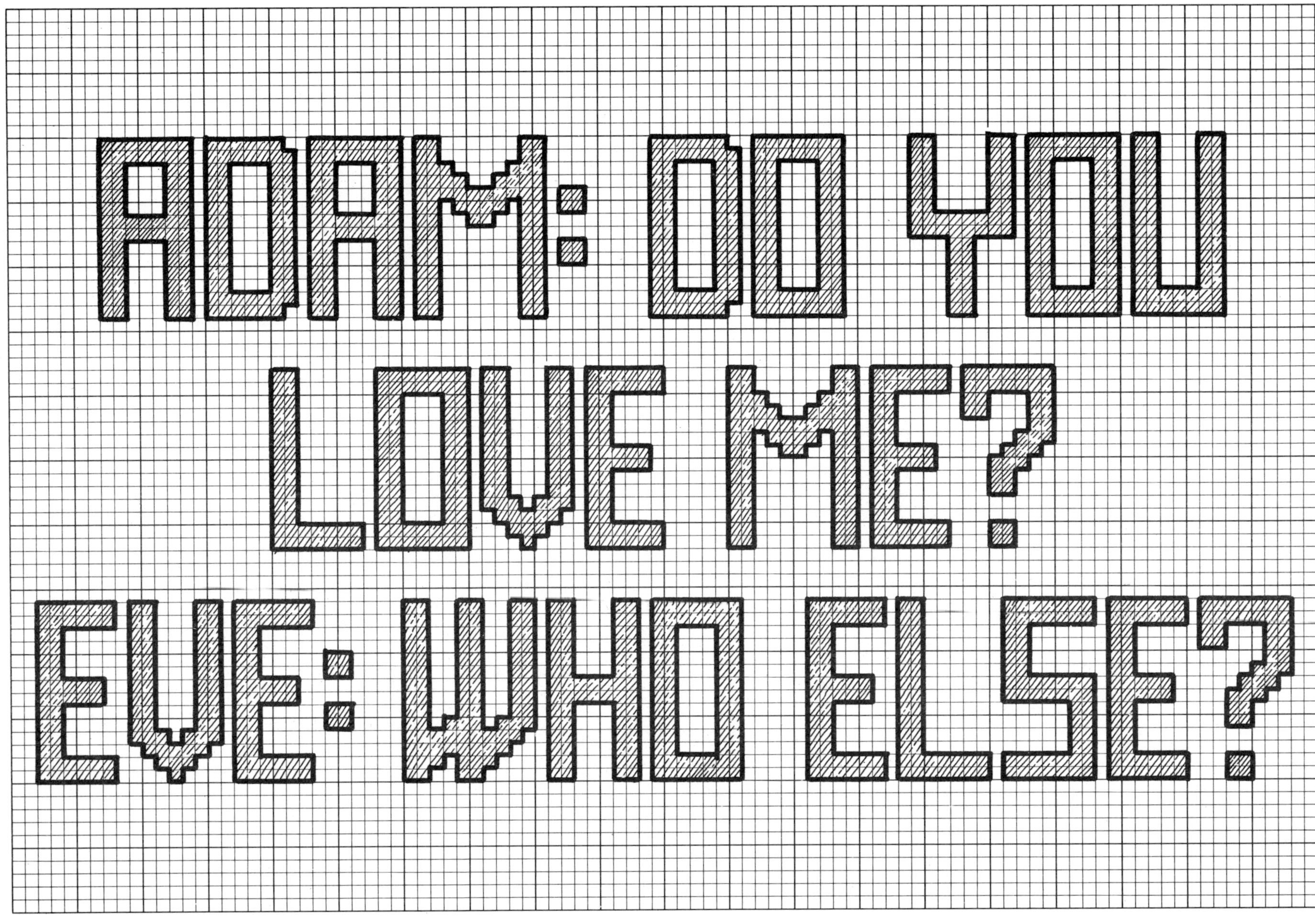
ADAM: DO YOU
LOVE ME?
EVE: WHO ELSE?

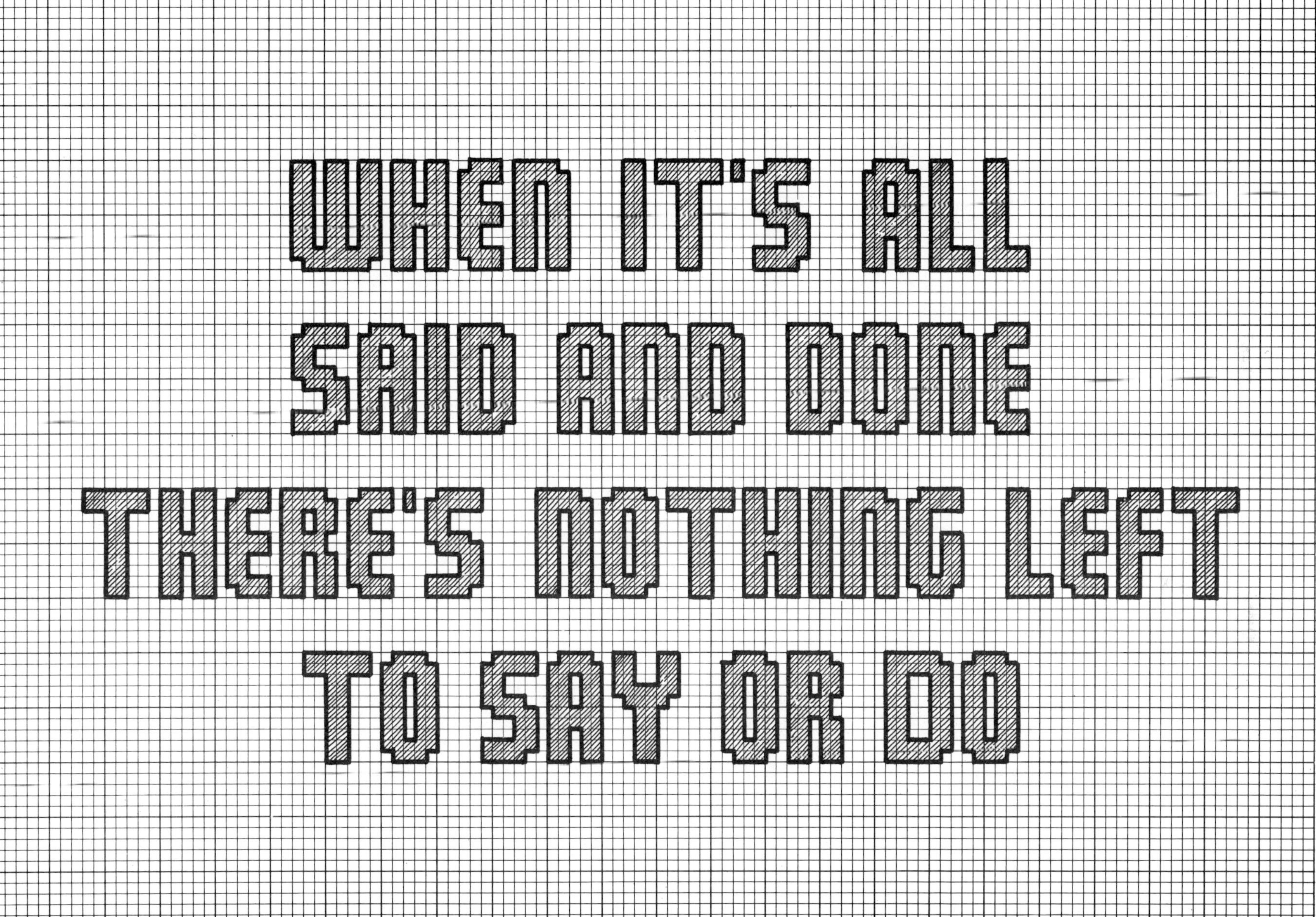
WHEN IT'S ALL
SAID AND DONE
THERE'S NOTHING LEFT
TO SAY OR DO

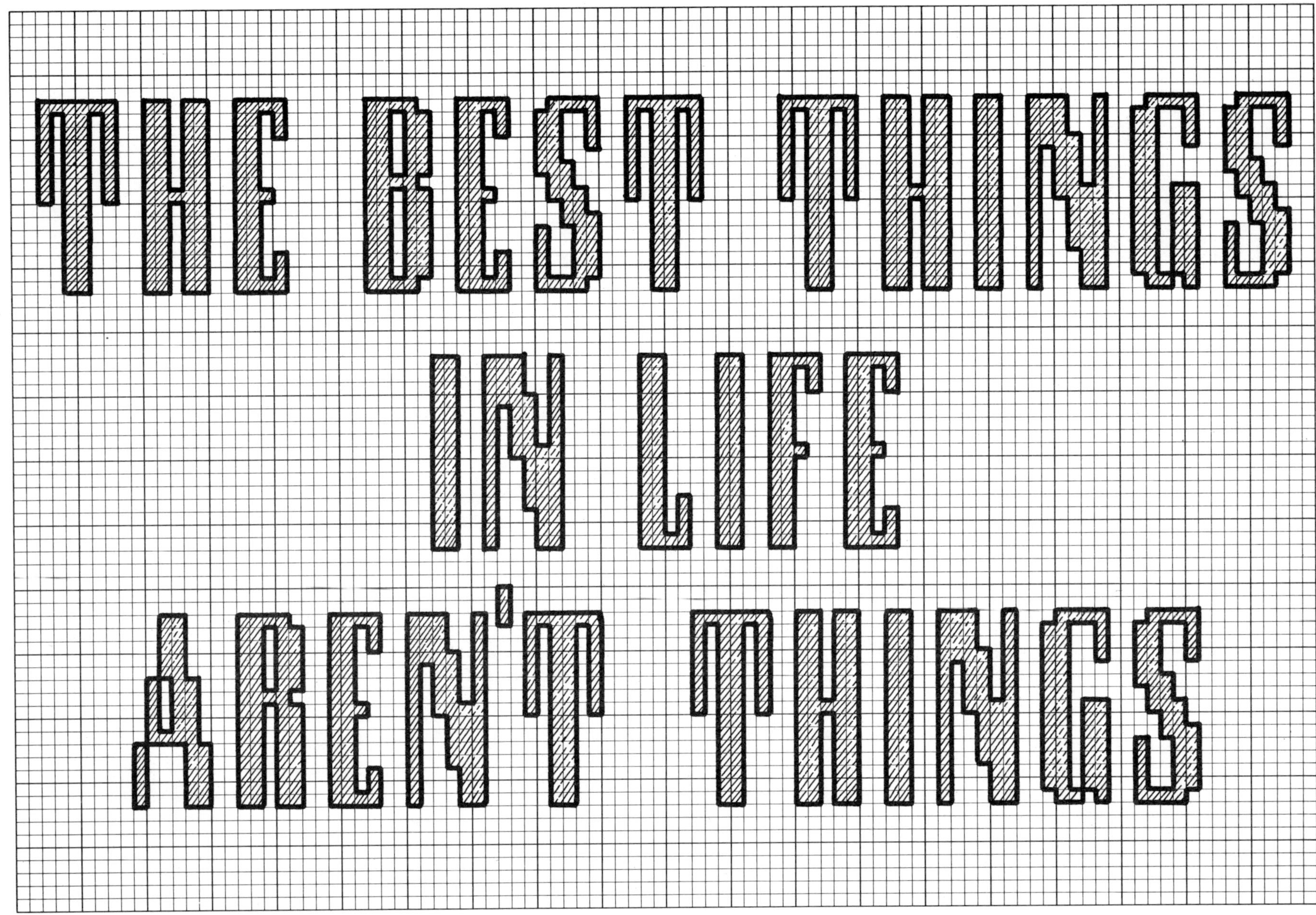
THE BEST THINGS
IN LIFE
AREN'T THINGS

REAL MEN
DON'T HAVE
FLOPPY DISKS

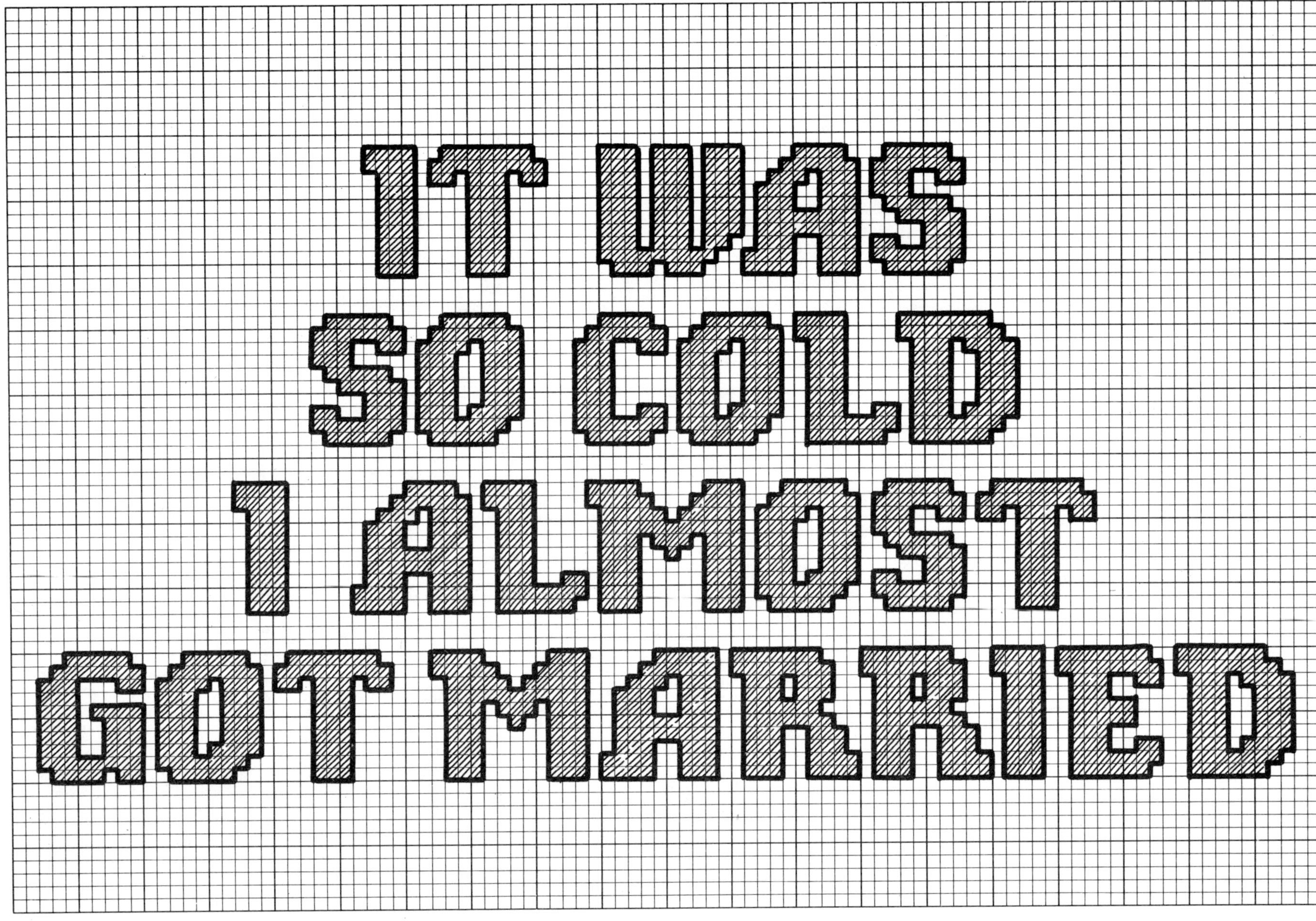
IT WAS
SO COLD
I ALMOST
GOT MARRIED

THIS IS NO
DRESS REHEARSAL-
THIS IS IT

HE WHO
LAUGHS
LASTS

ONCE
I THOUGHT
I WAS WRONG-
BUT I WAS
MISTAKEN

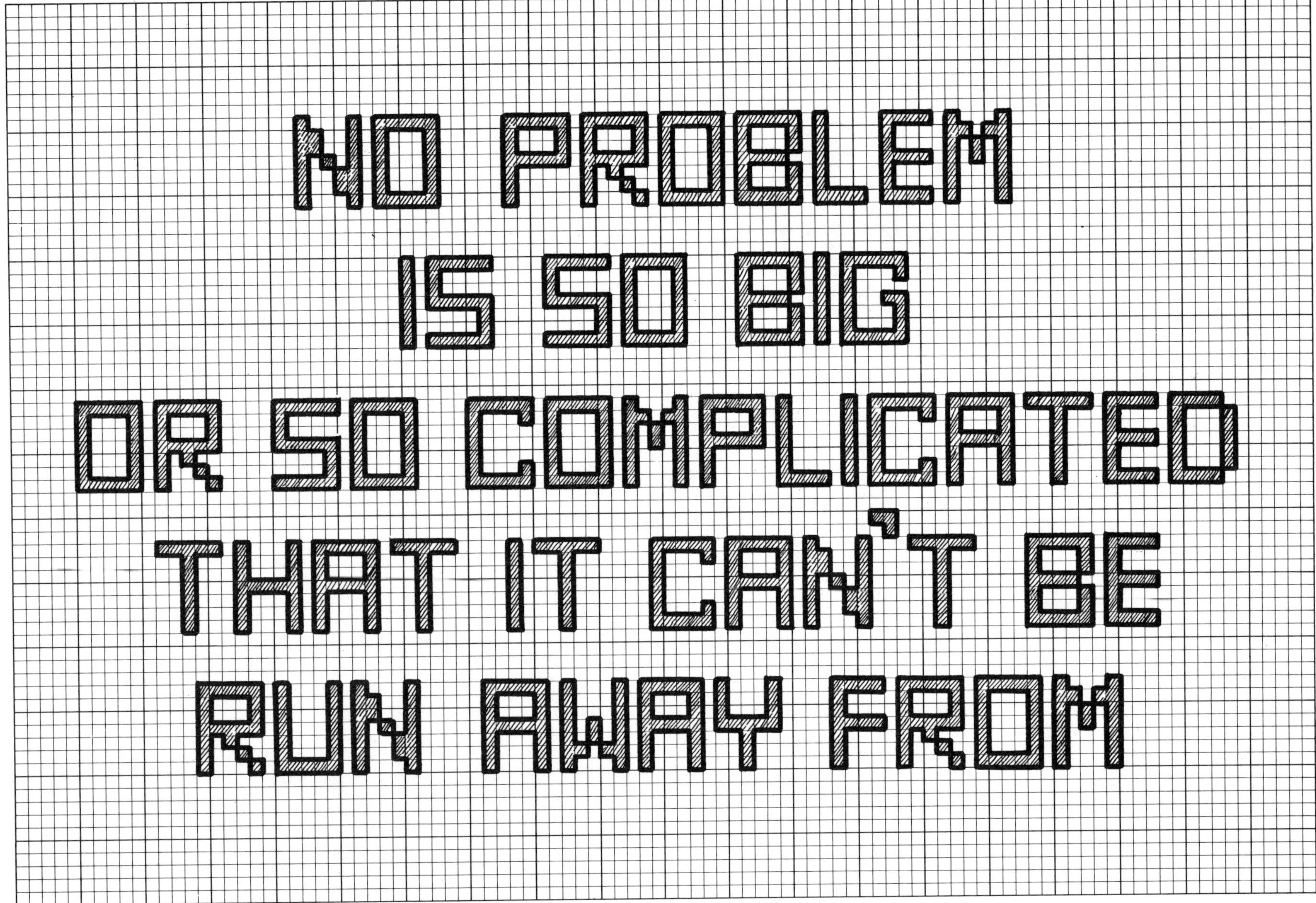
NO PROBLEM
IS SO BIG
OR SO COMPLICATED
THAT IT CAN'T BE
RUN AWAY FROM

YOU'VE GOT
A LOT OF
CHUTZPAH

I'M THE
MOMMY,
THAT'S WHY

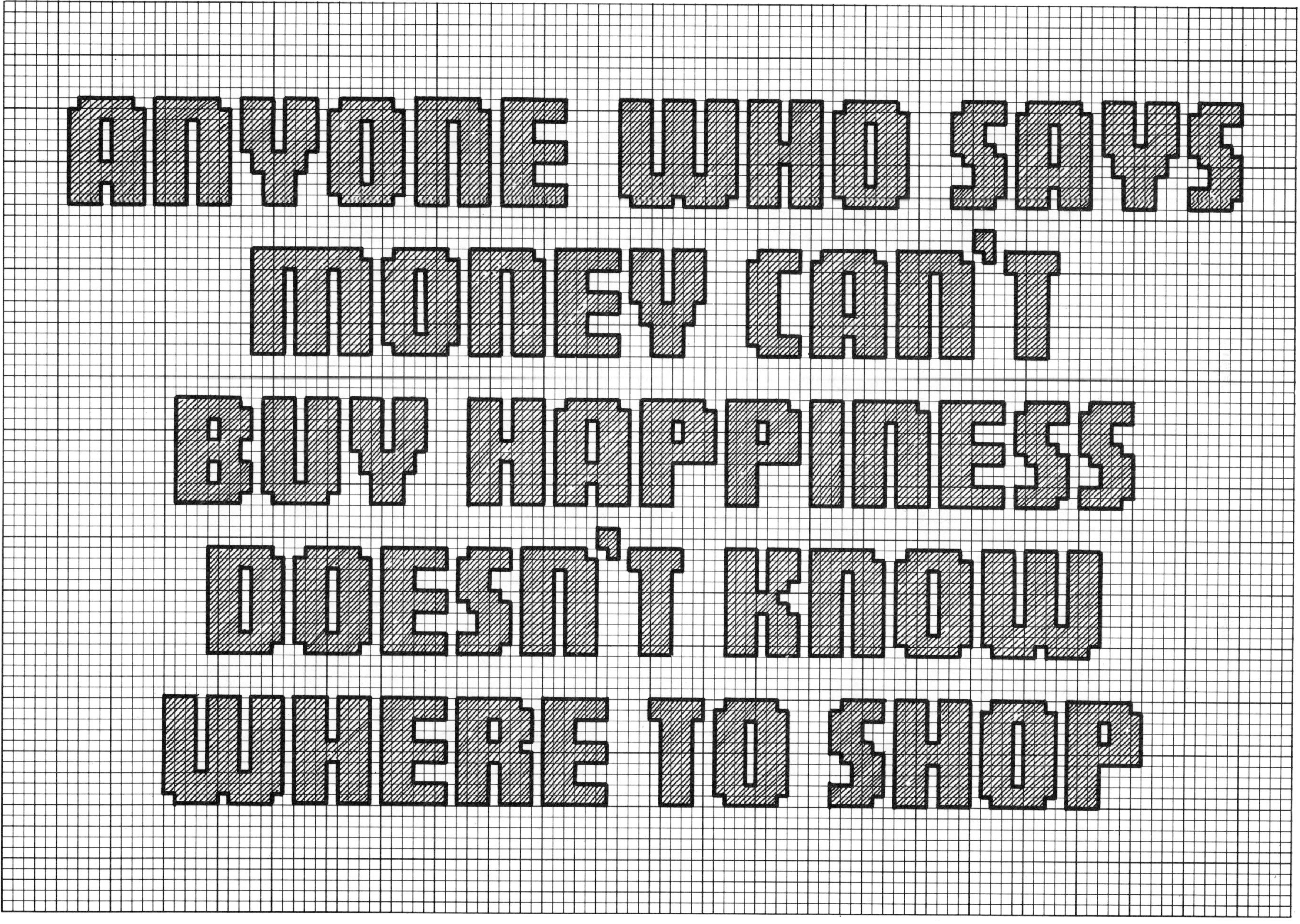
ANYONE WHO SAYS
MONEY CAN'T
BUY HAPPINESS
DOESN'T KNOW
WHERE TO SHOP

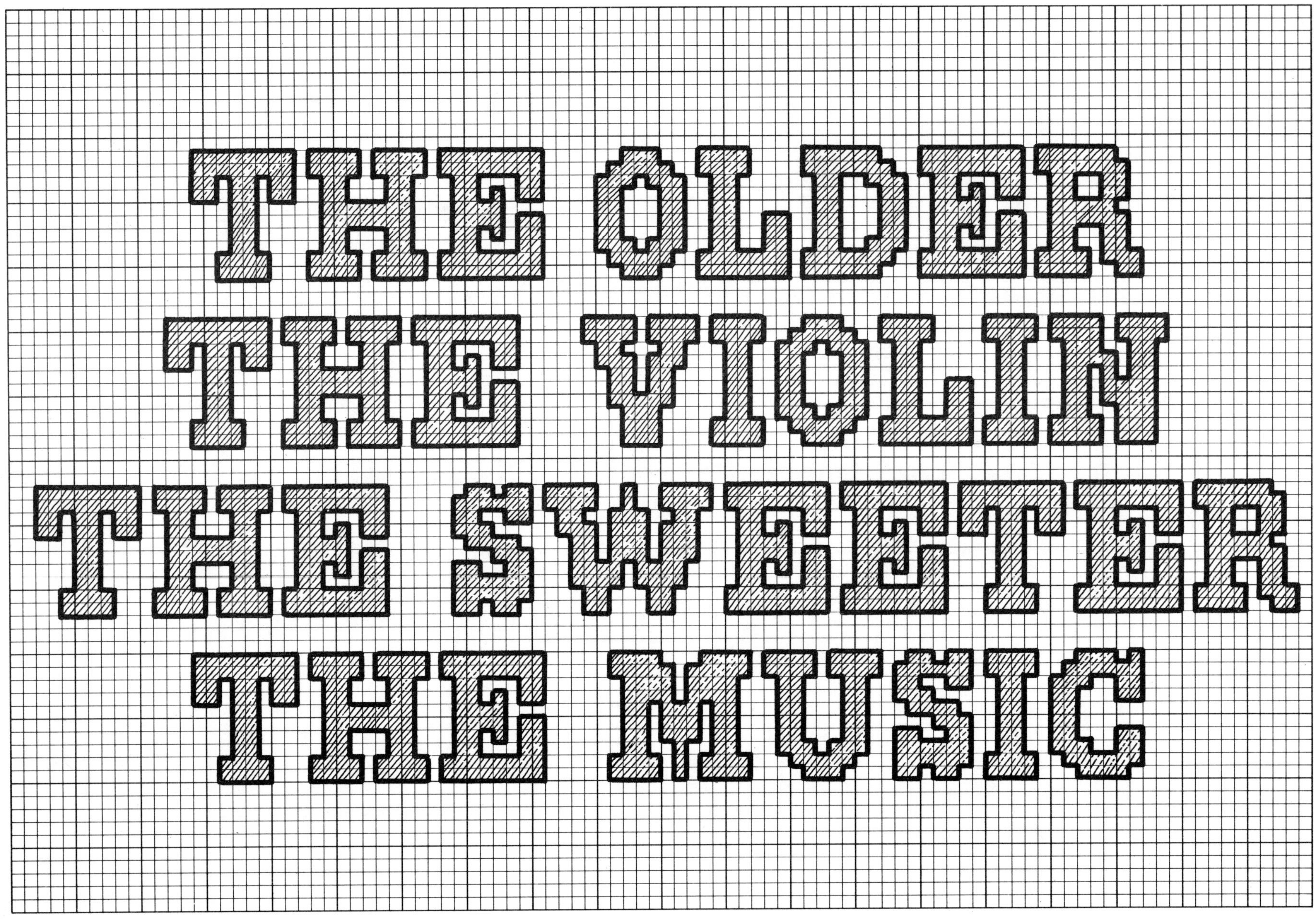
THE OLDER
THE VIOLIN
THE SWEETER
THE MUSIC

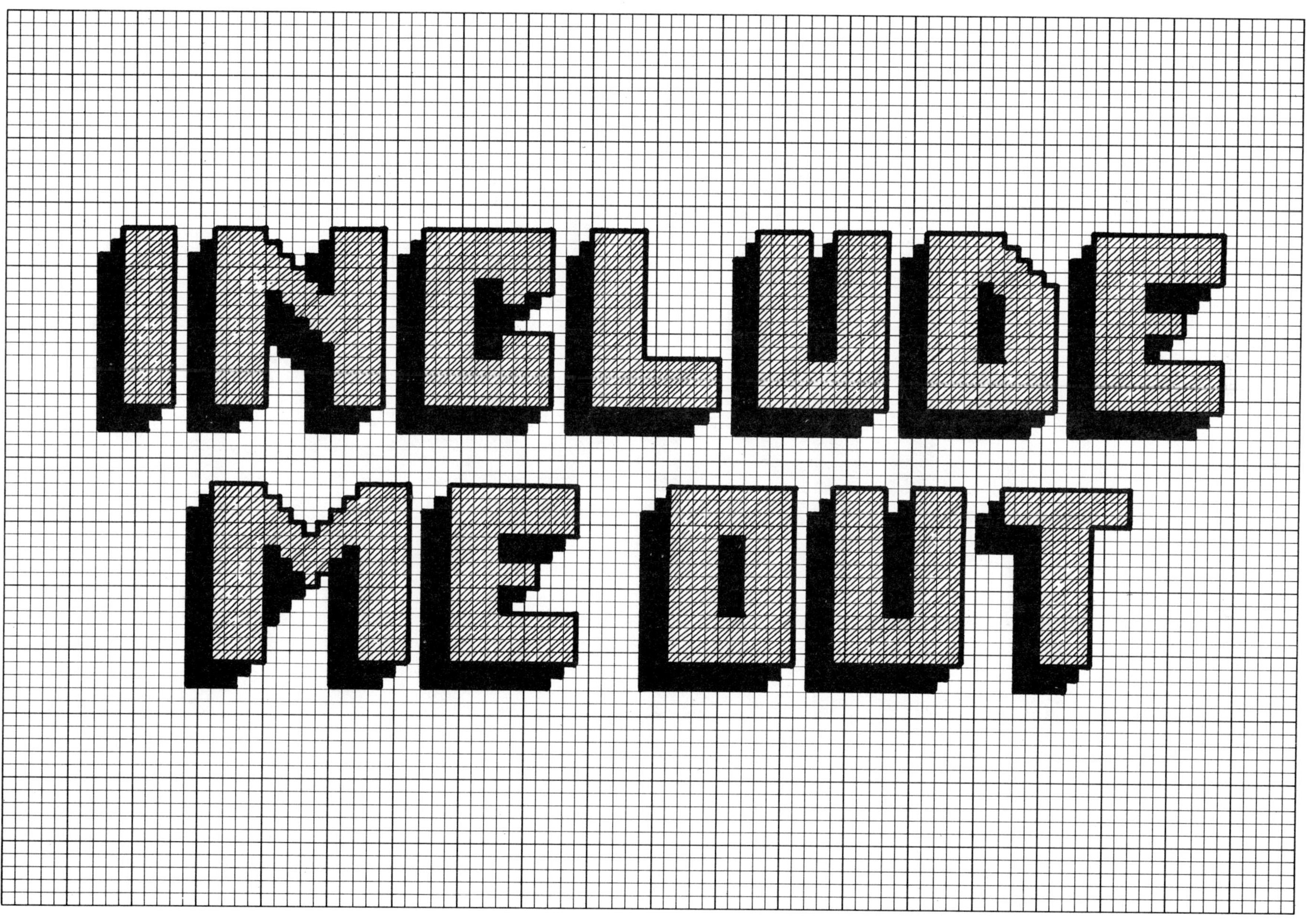
INCLUDE
ME OUT

THE
GODDESS
SLEEPS HERE

MOTHER
KNOWS
BEST

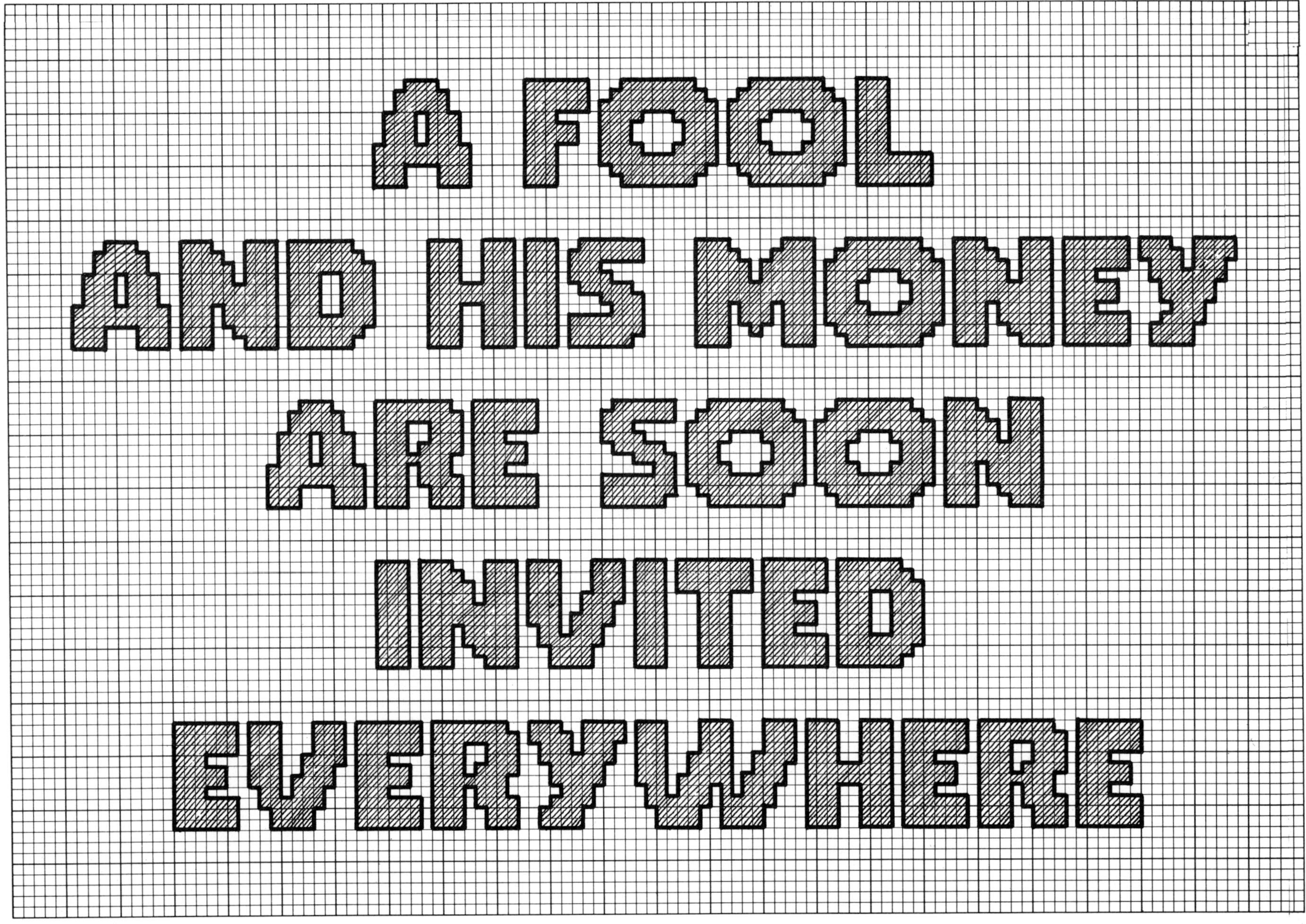
A FOOL
AND HIS MONEY
ARE SOON
INVITED
EVERYWHERE

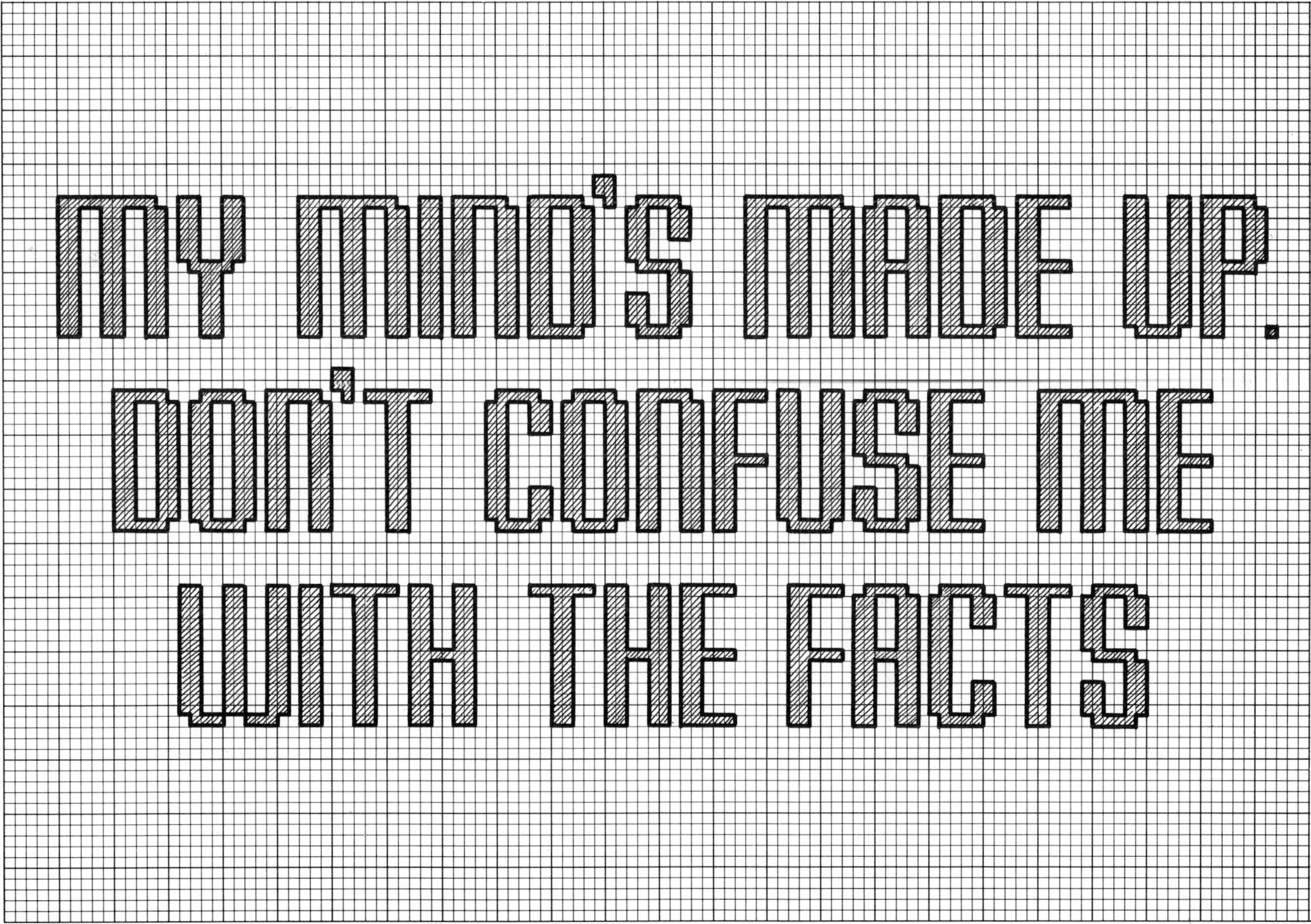
MY MIND'S MADE UP.
DON'T CONFUSE ME
WITH THE FACTS

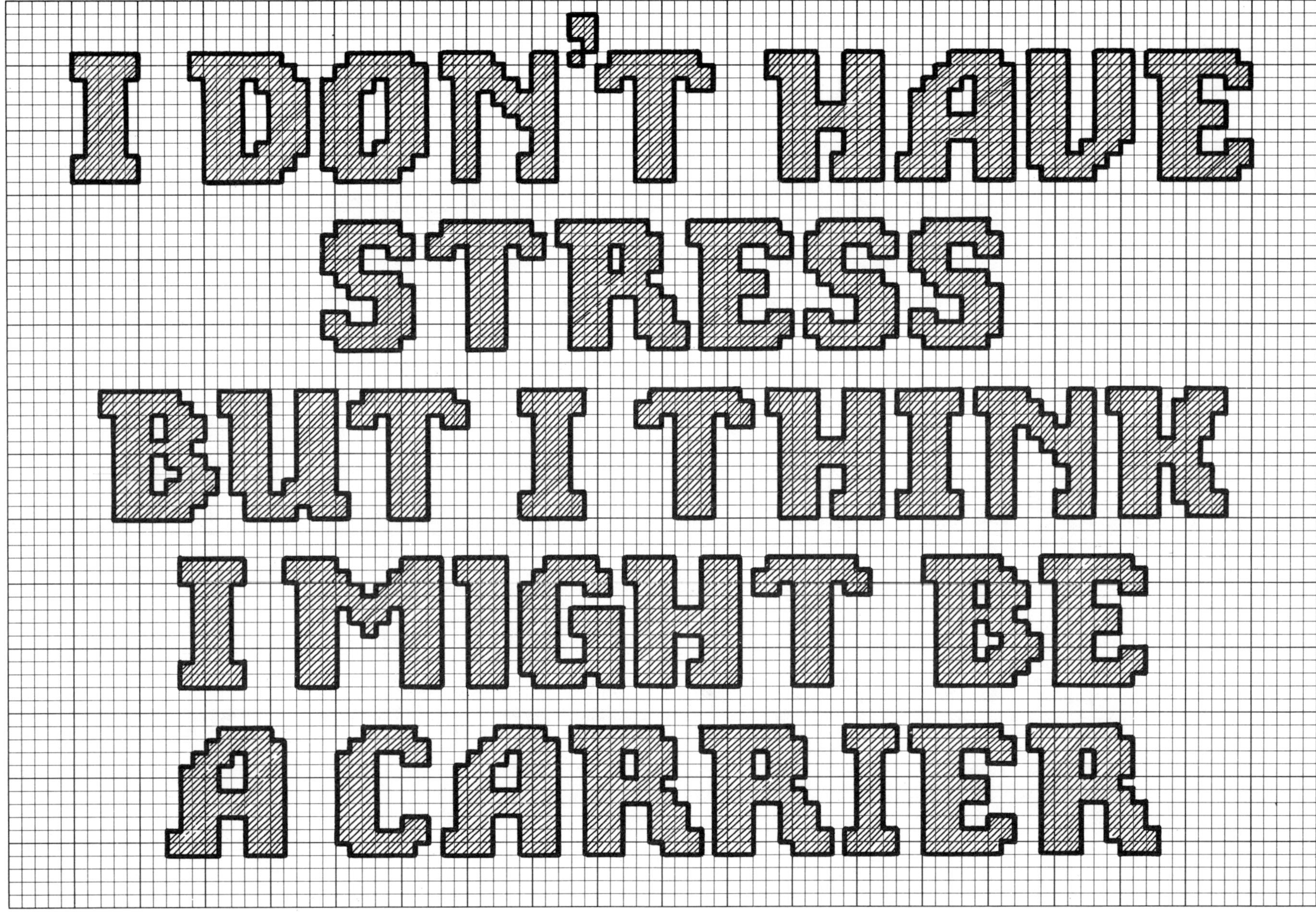
I DON'T HAVE
STRESS
BUT I THINK
I MIGHT BE
A CARRIER

GO FOR IT

WHEN MY SHIP
COMES IN
I'LL PROBABLY
BE WAITING
AT THE AIRPORT

MY MAMMA
DIDN'T RAISE
NO FOOL

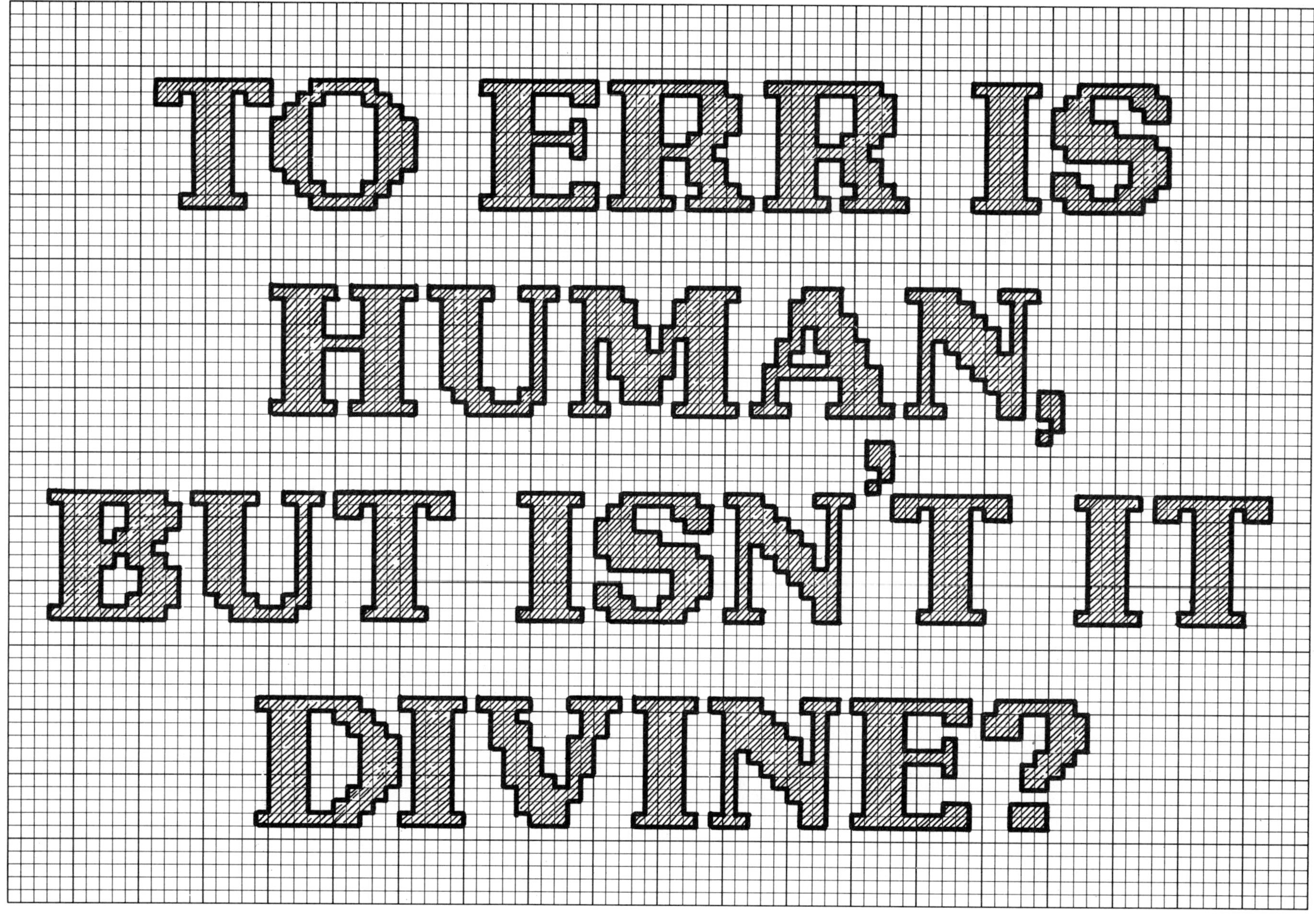
TO ERR IS
HUMAN,
BUT ISN'T IT
DIVINE?

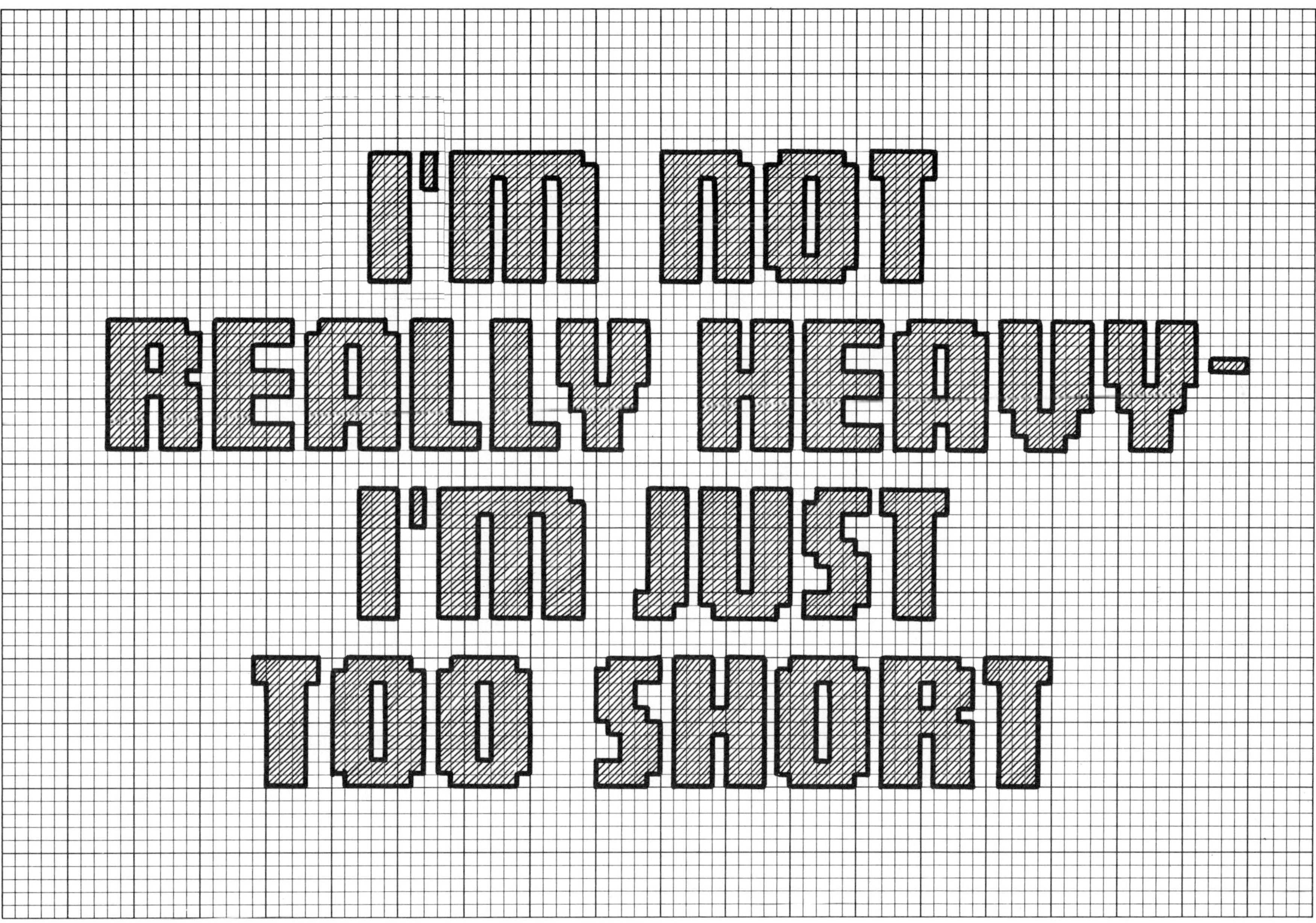
I'M NOT
REALLY HEAVY-
I'M JUST
TOO SHORT

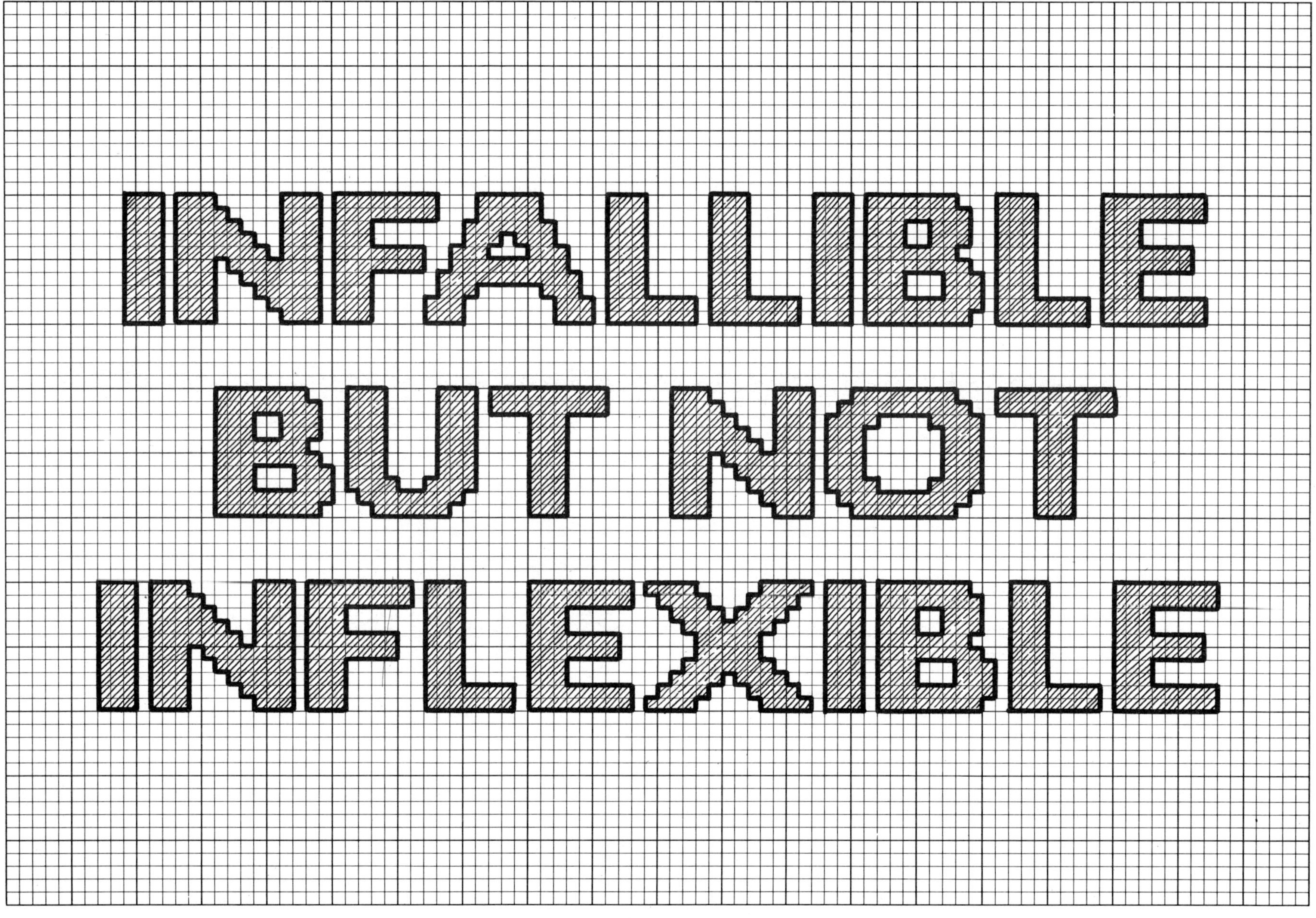
INFALLIBLE
BUT NOT
INFLEXIBLE

THE BEST MAN
FOR THE JOB
IS A WOMAN

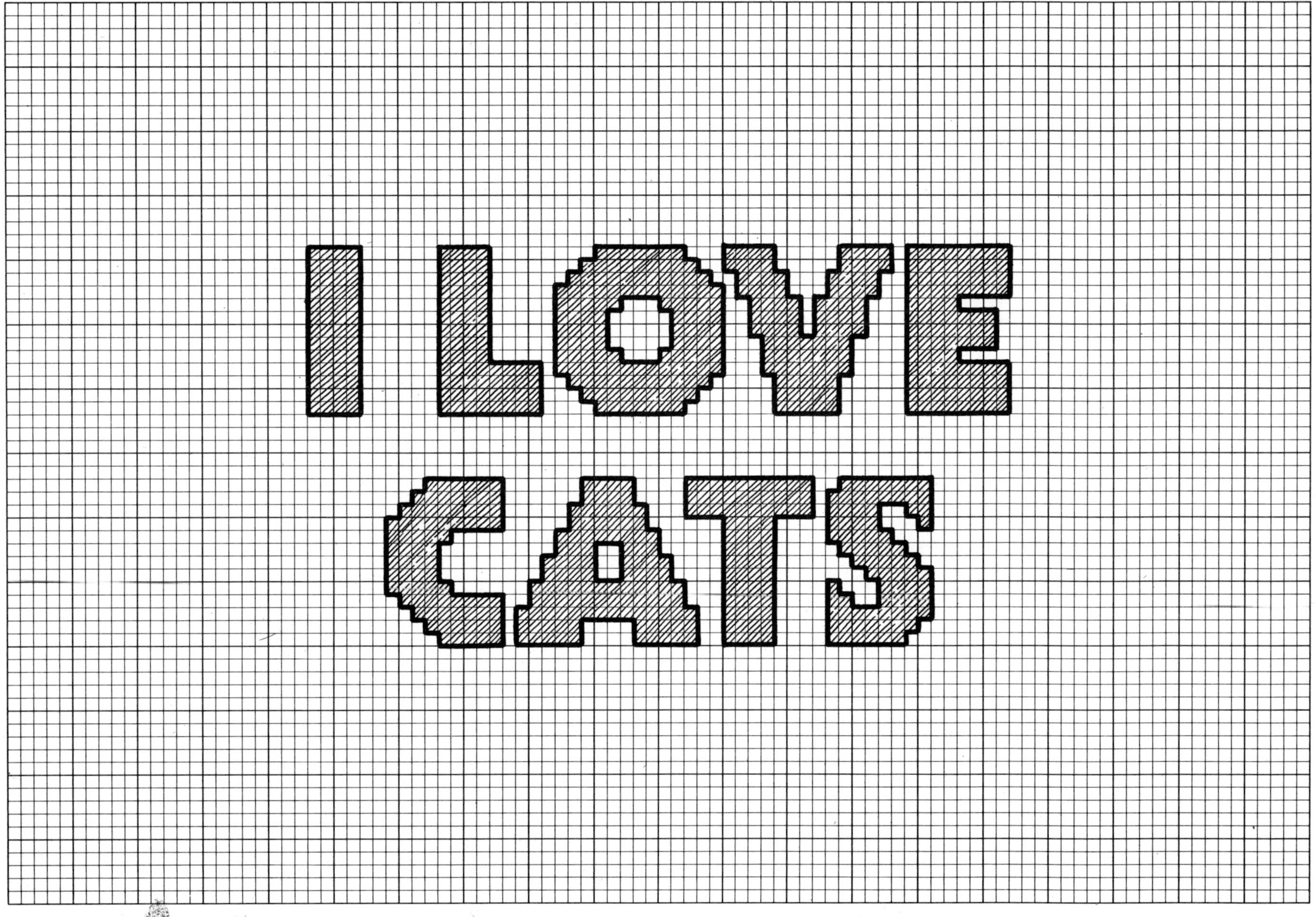
I LOVE
CATS

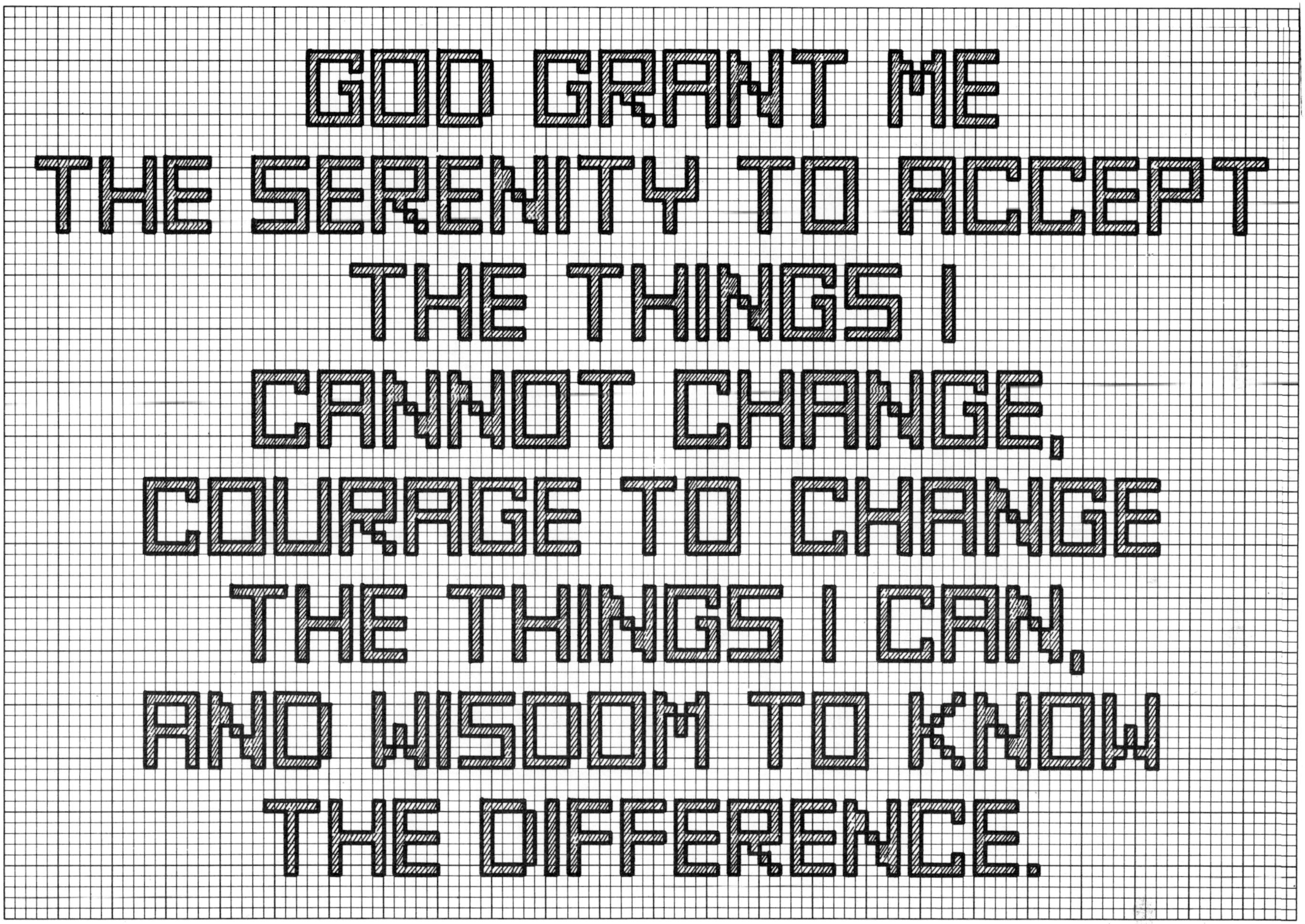

GOD GRANT ME
THE SERENITY TO ACCEPT
THE THINGS I
CANNOT CHANGE,
COURAGE TO CHANGE
THE THINGS I CAN,
AND WISDOM TO KNOW
THE DIFFERENCE.

NONE
FOR THE
ROAD

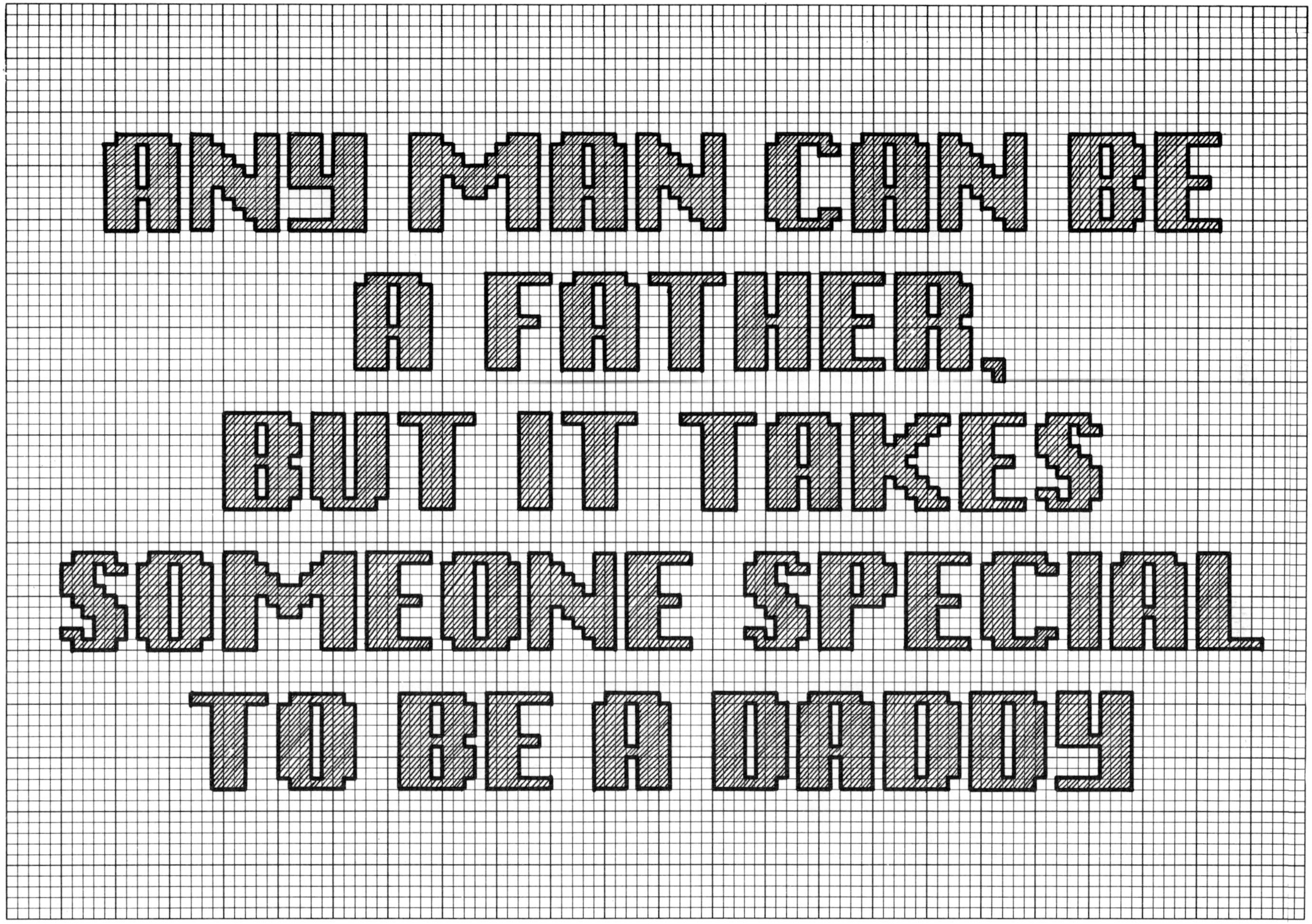

ANY MAN CAN BE
A FATHER,
BUT IT TAKES
SOMEONE SPECIAL
TO BE A DADDY

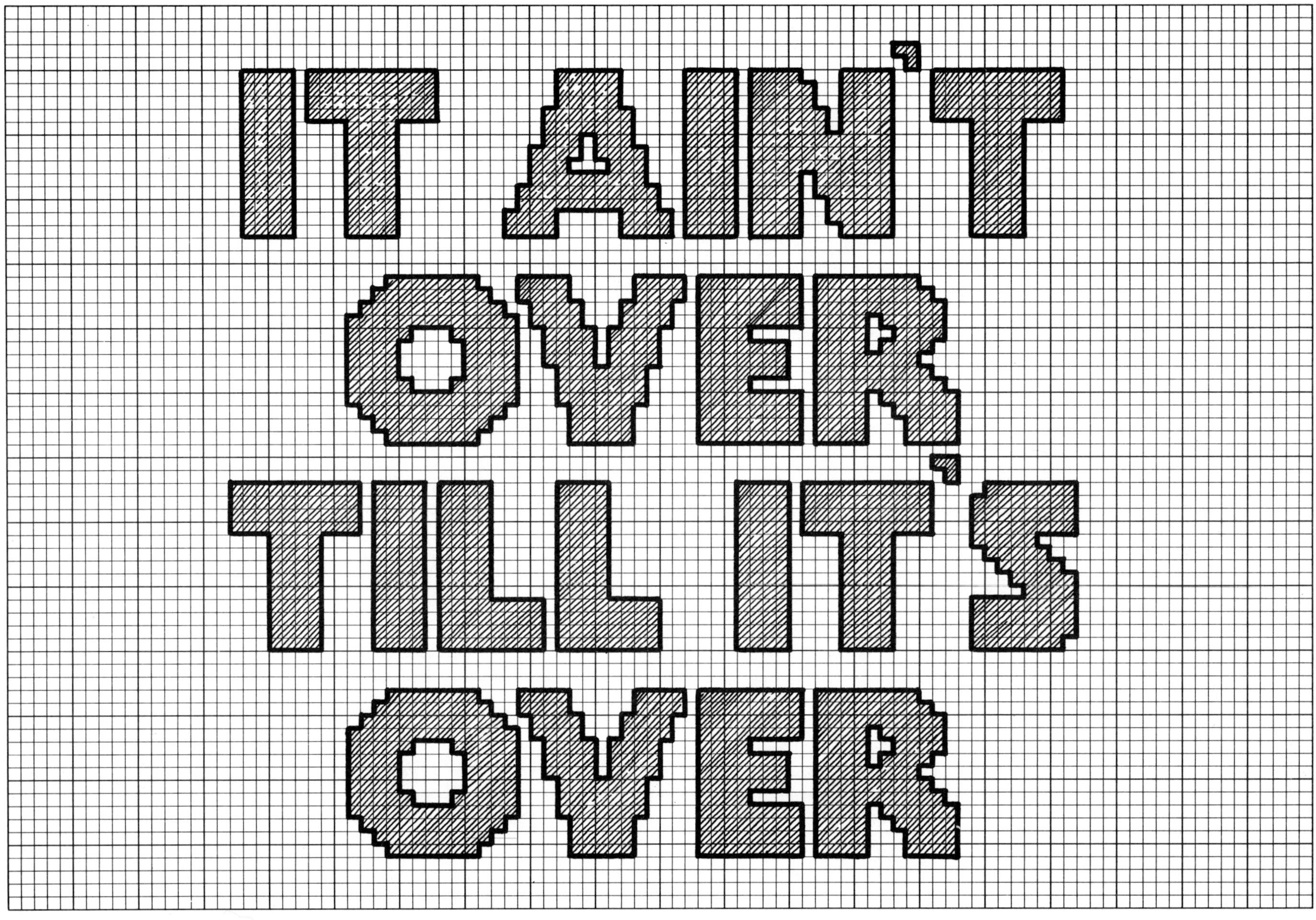
IT AIN'T
OVER
TILL IT'S
OVER

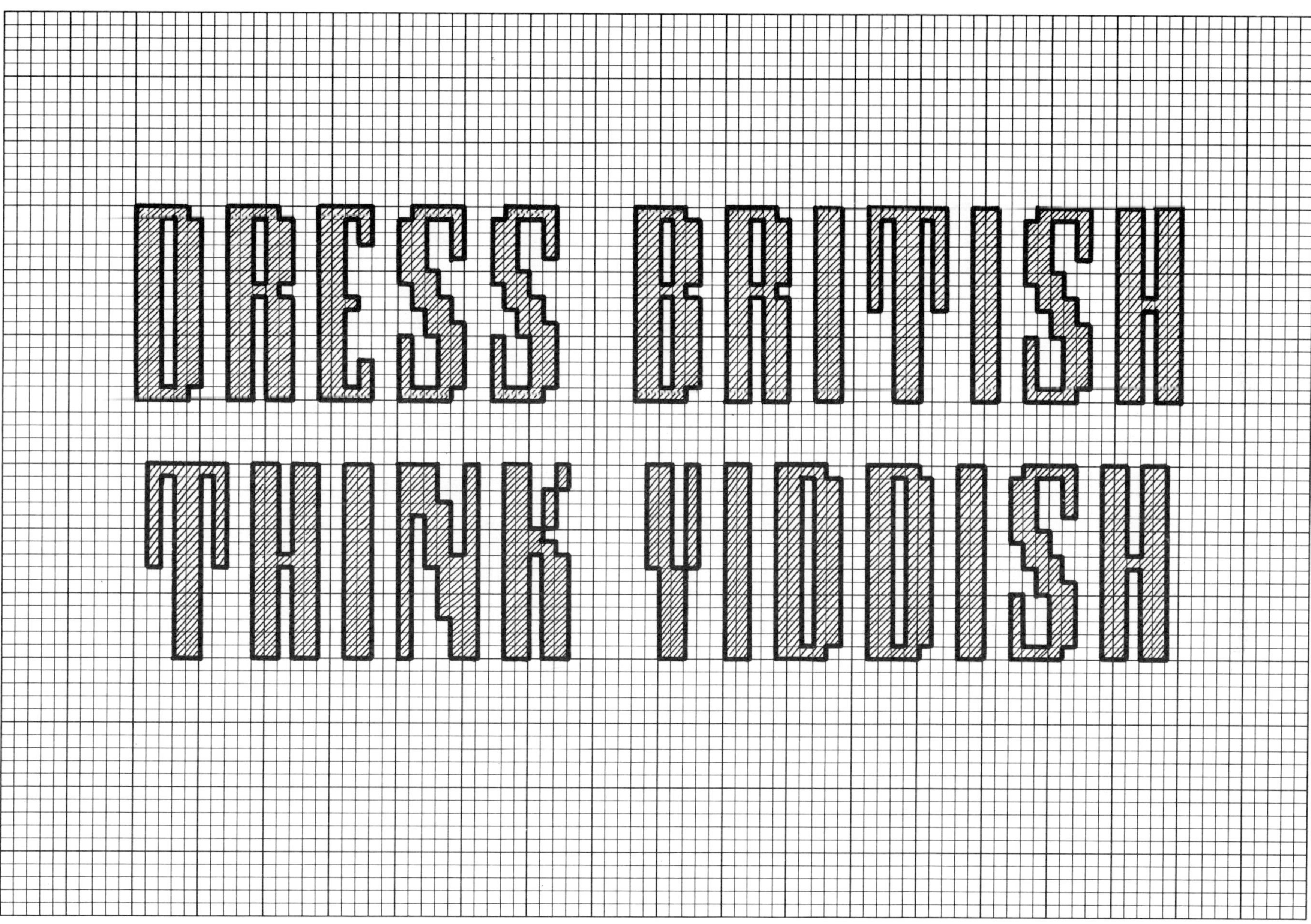
DRESS BRITISH
THINK YIDDISH

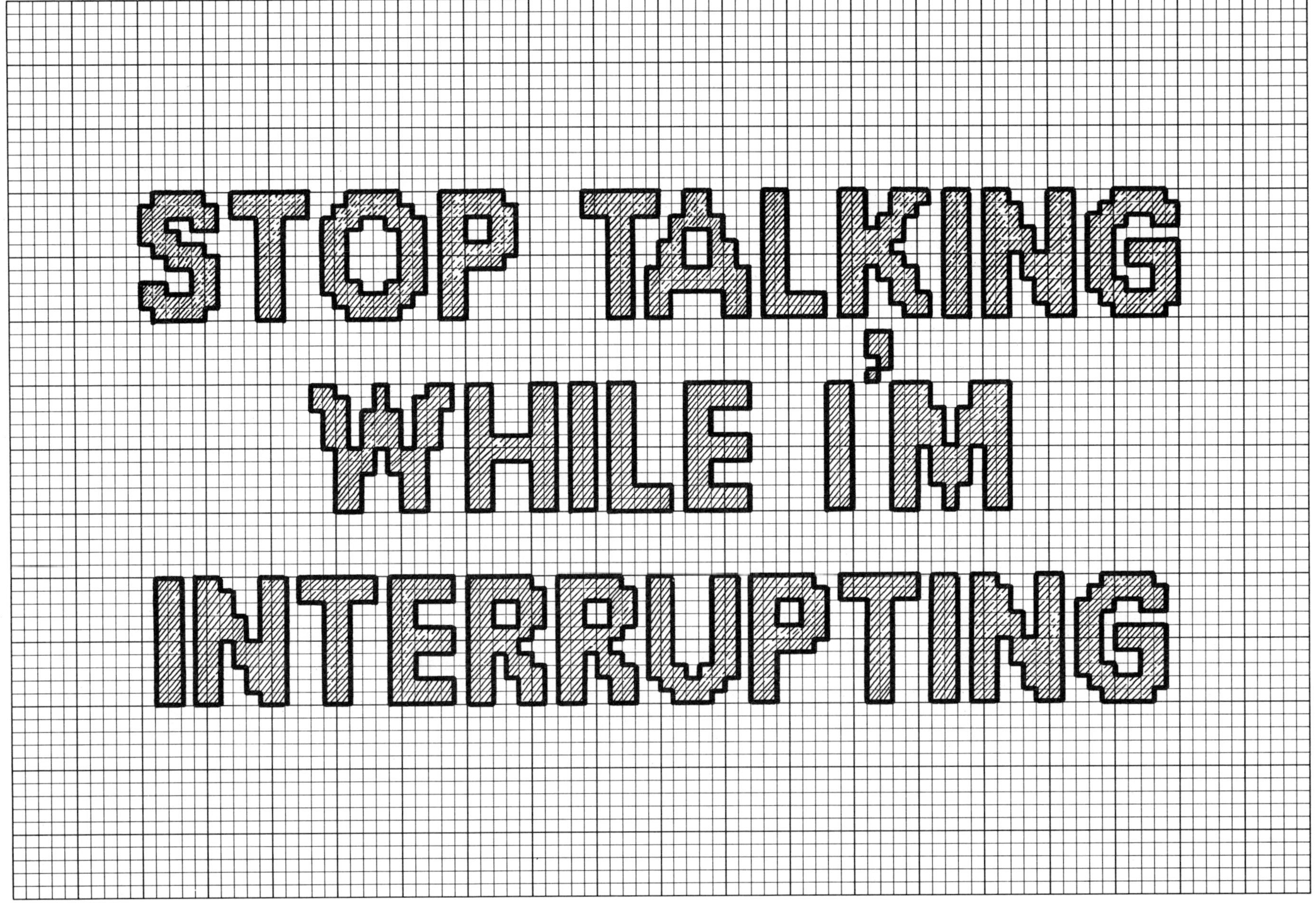
STOP TALKING
WHILE I'M
INTERRUPTING

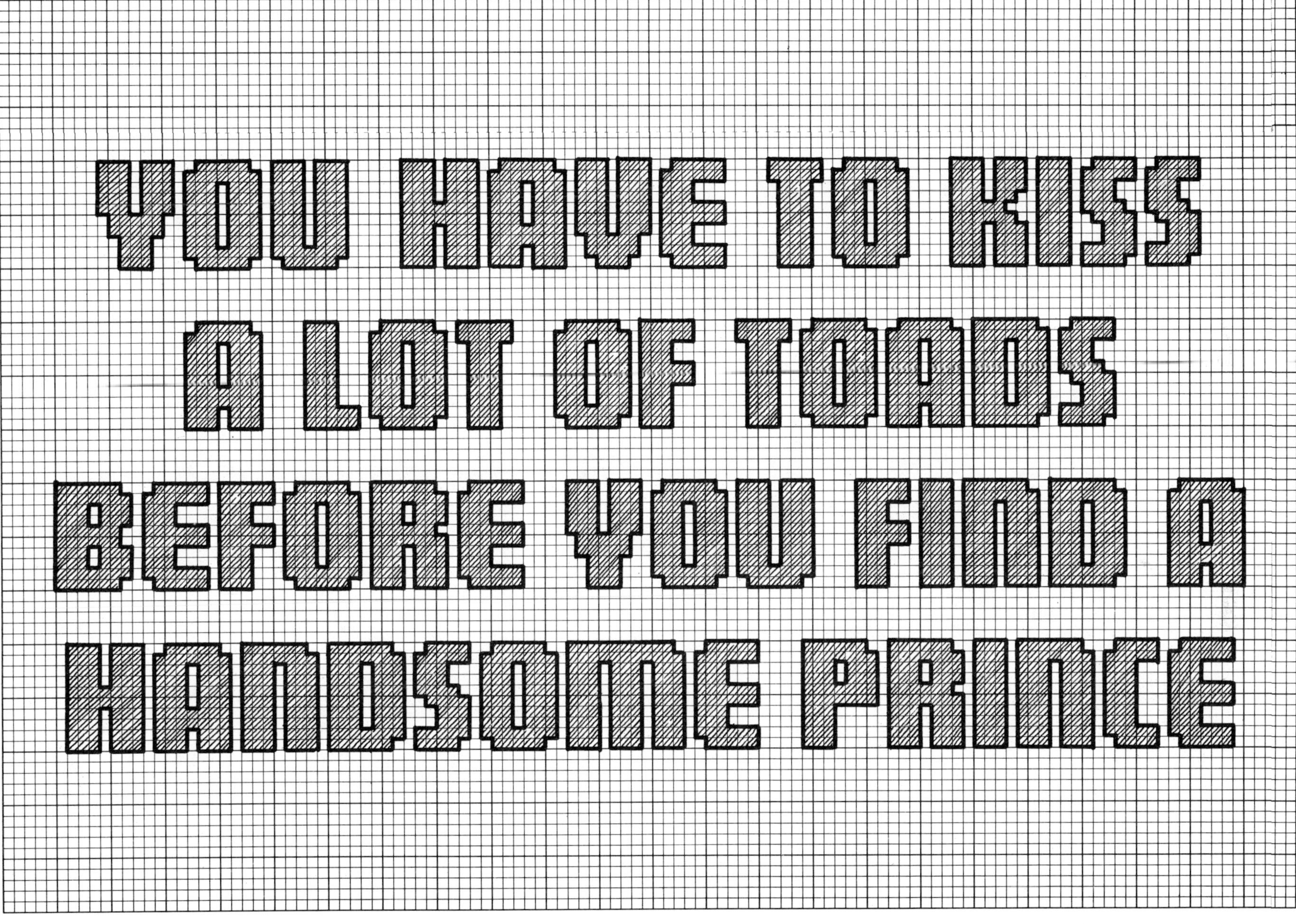
YOU HAVE TO KISS
A LOT OF TOADS
BEFORE YOU FIND A
HANDSOME PRINCE

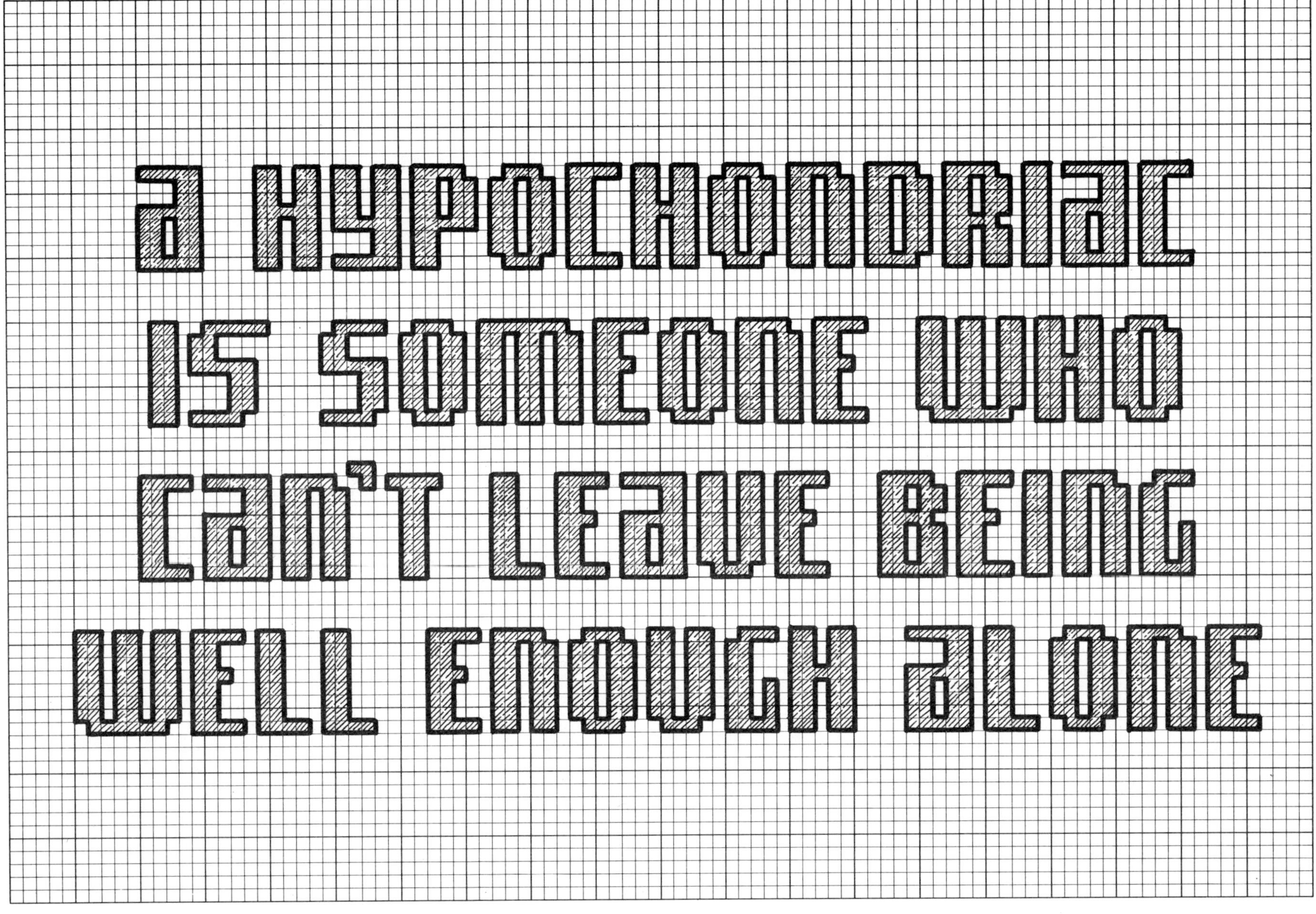
A HYPOCHONDRIAC
IS SOMEONE WHO
CAN'T LEAVE BEING
WELL ENOUGH ALONE

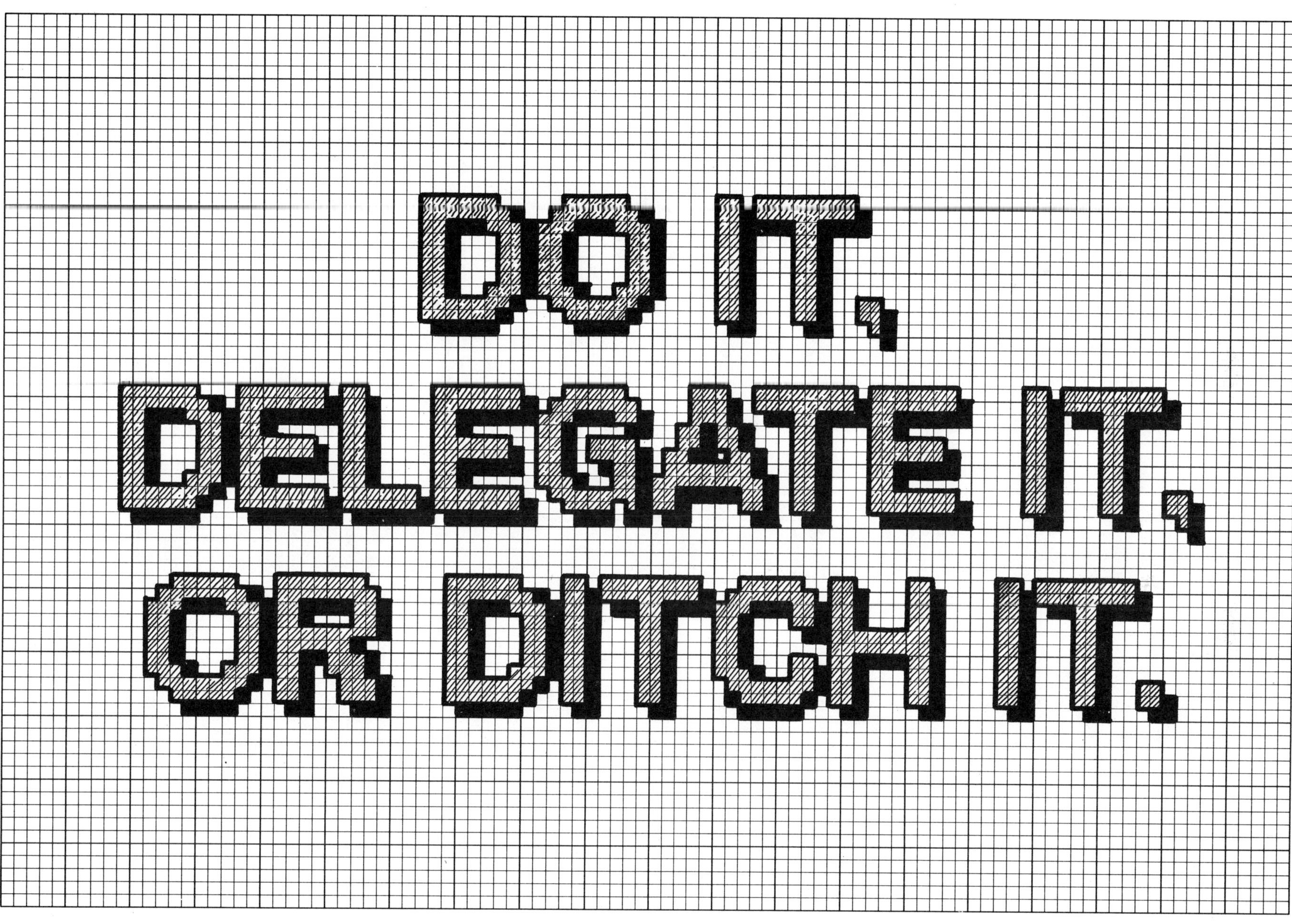
DO IT,
DELEGATE IT,
OR DITCH IT.

I AM EASILY
SATISFIED
WITH THE
VERY BEST

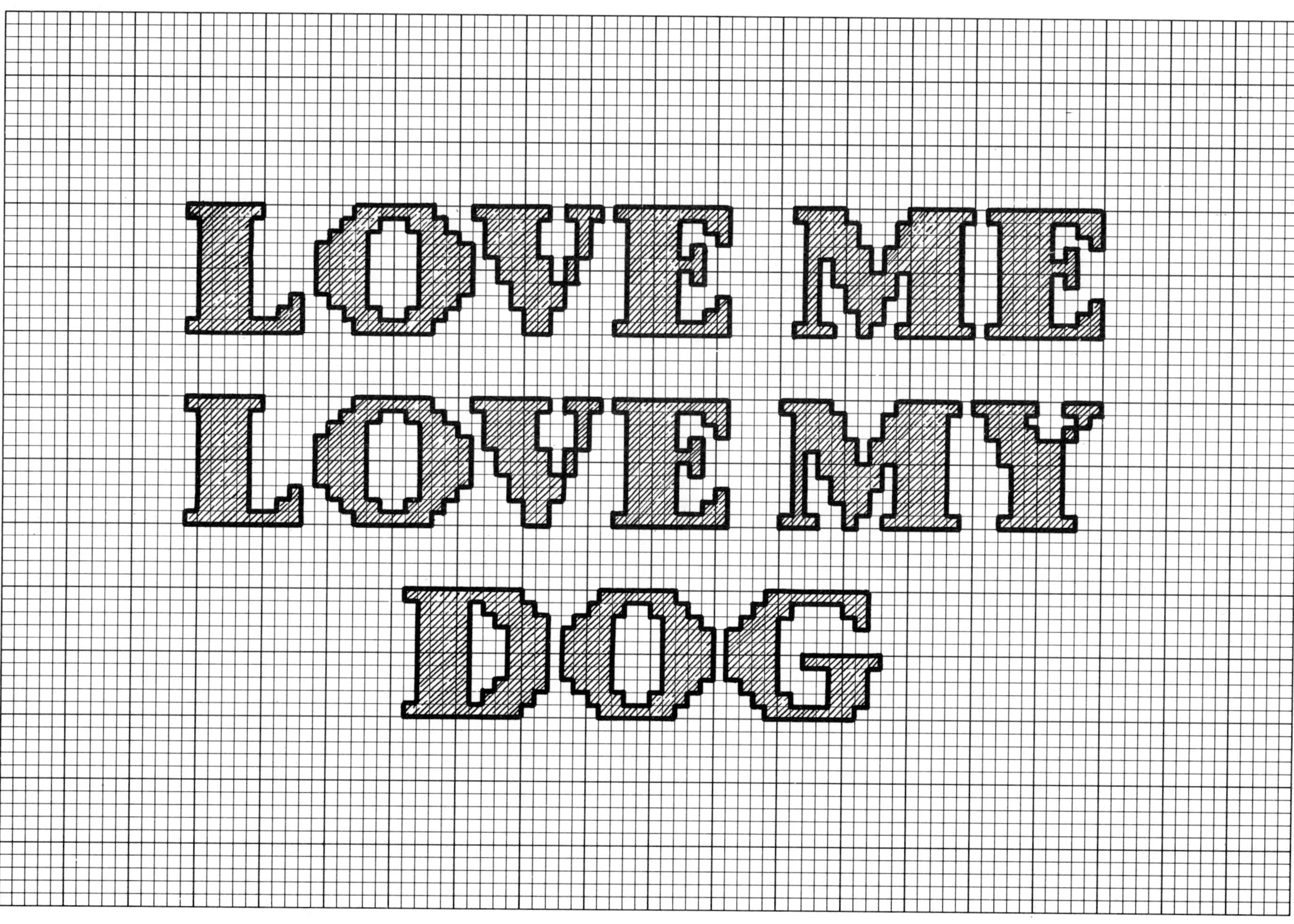
LOVE ME
LOVE MY
DOG

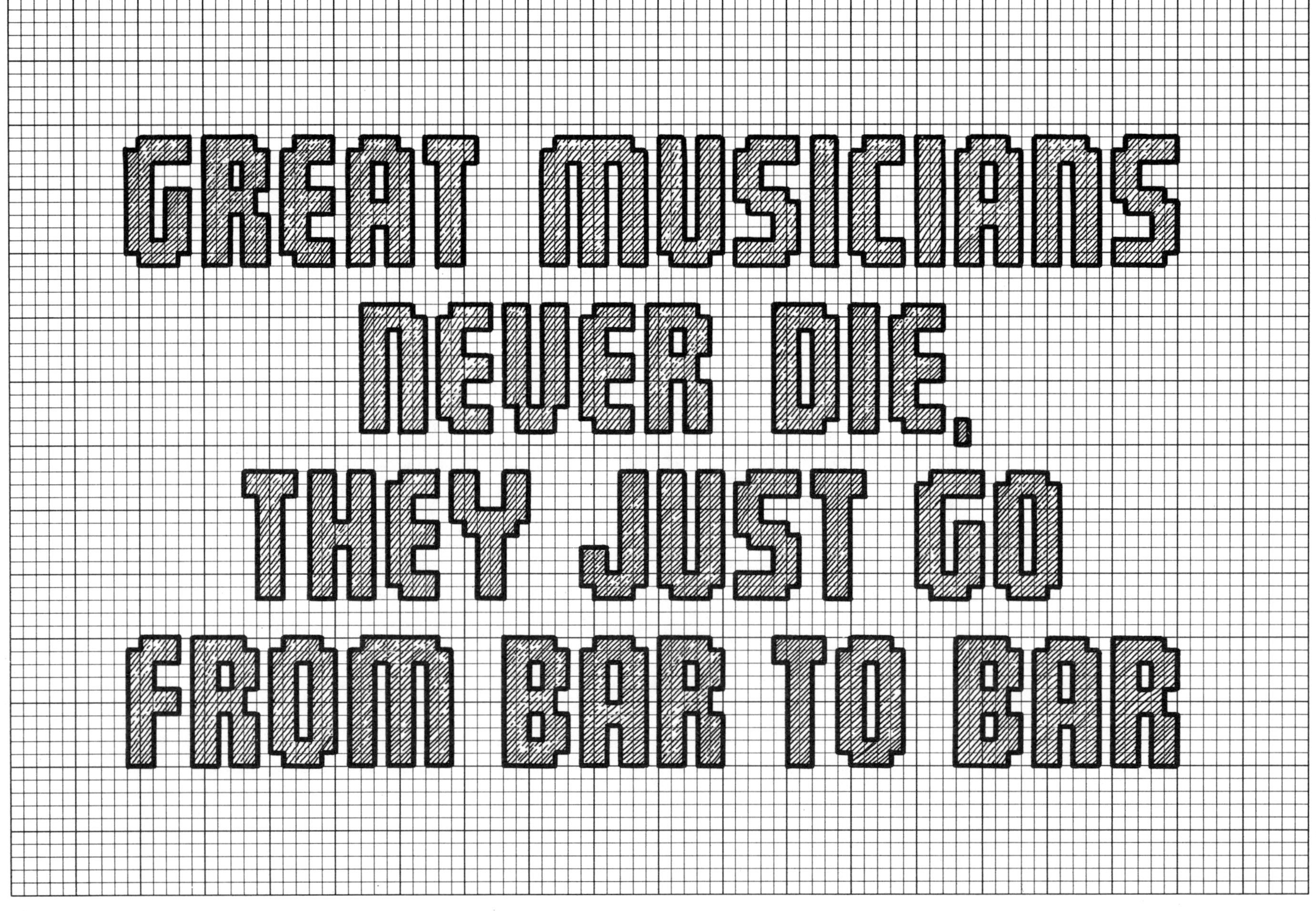
GREAT MUSICIANS
NEVER DIE,
THEY JUST GO
FROM BAR TO BAR

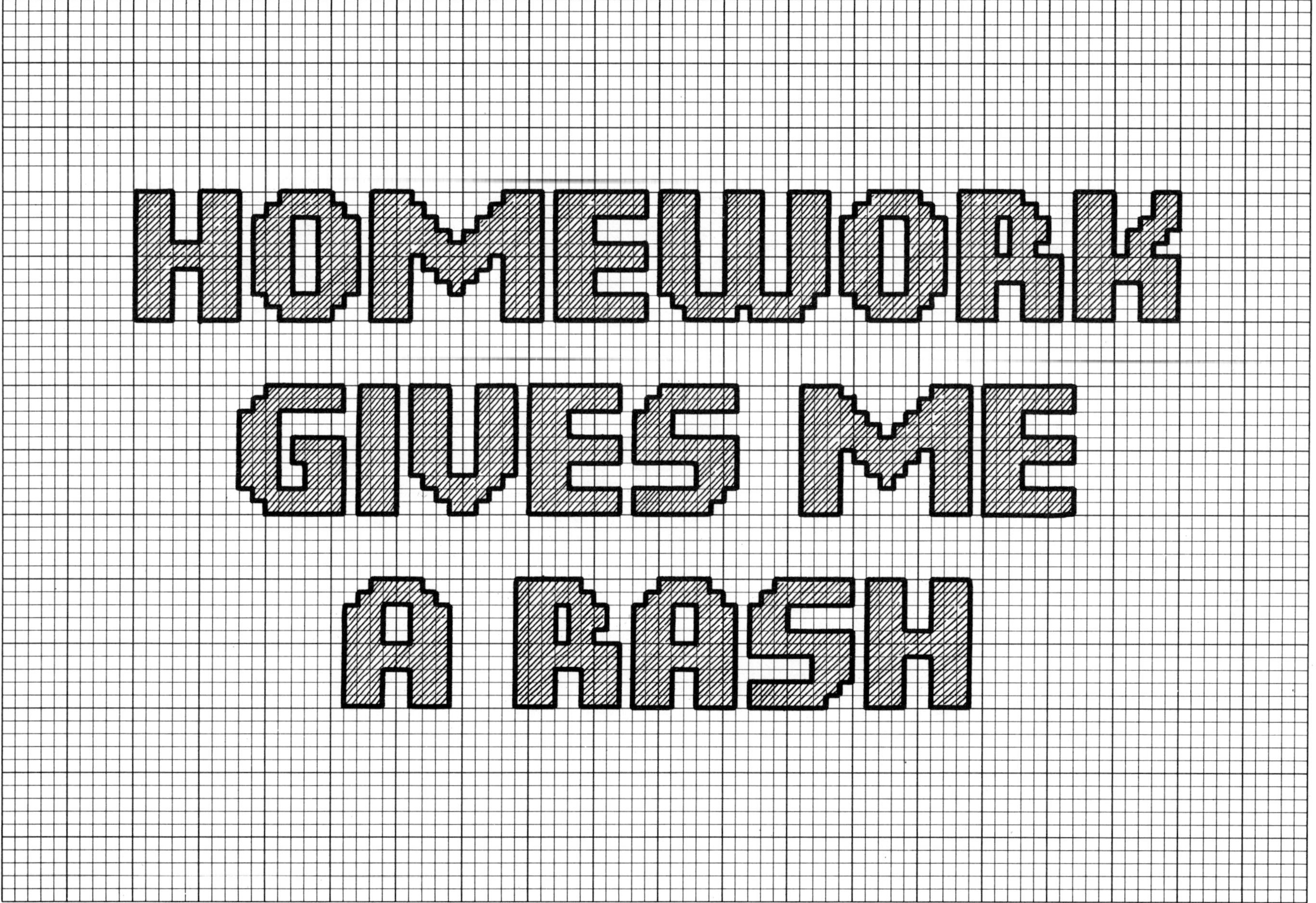
HOMEWORK
GIVES ME
A RASH

IS THIS
DEAL
KOSHER?

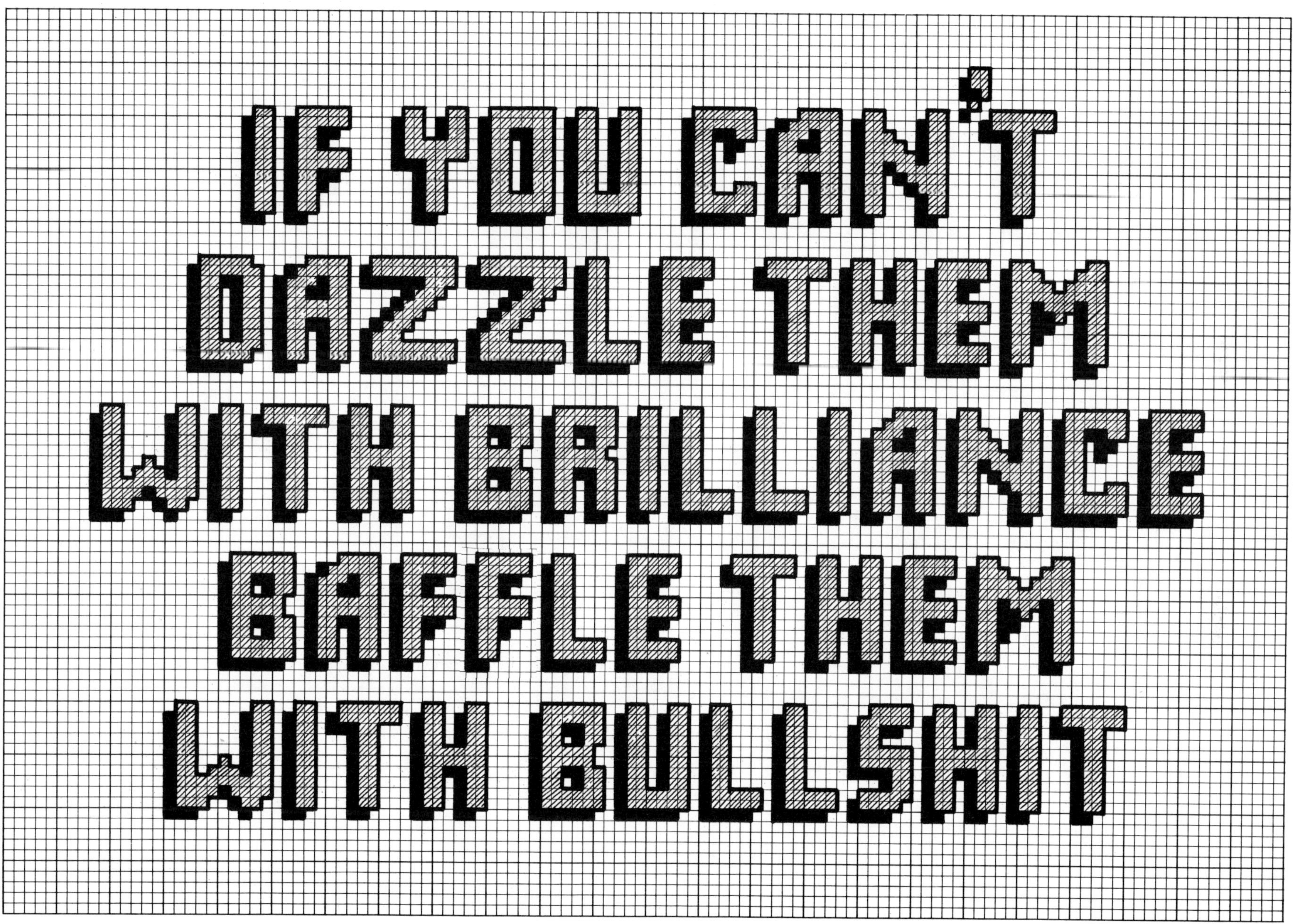
IF YOU CAN'T
DAZZLE THEM
WITH BRILLIANCE
BAFFLE THEM
WITH BULLSHIT

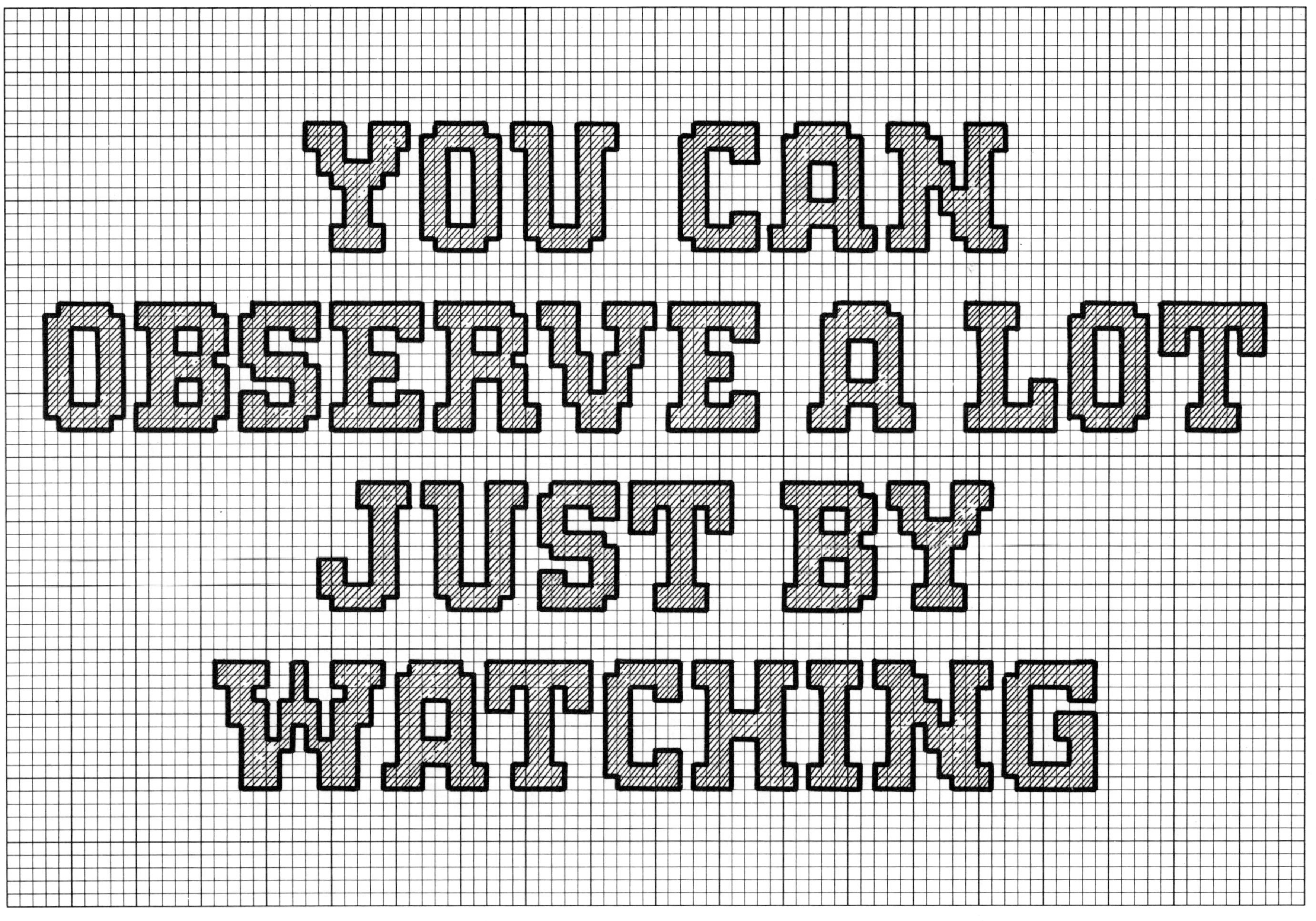
YOU CAN
OBSERVE A LOT
JUST BY
WATCHING

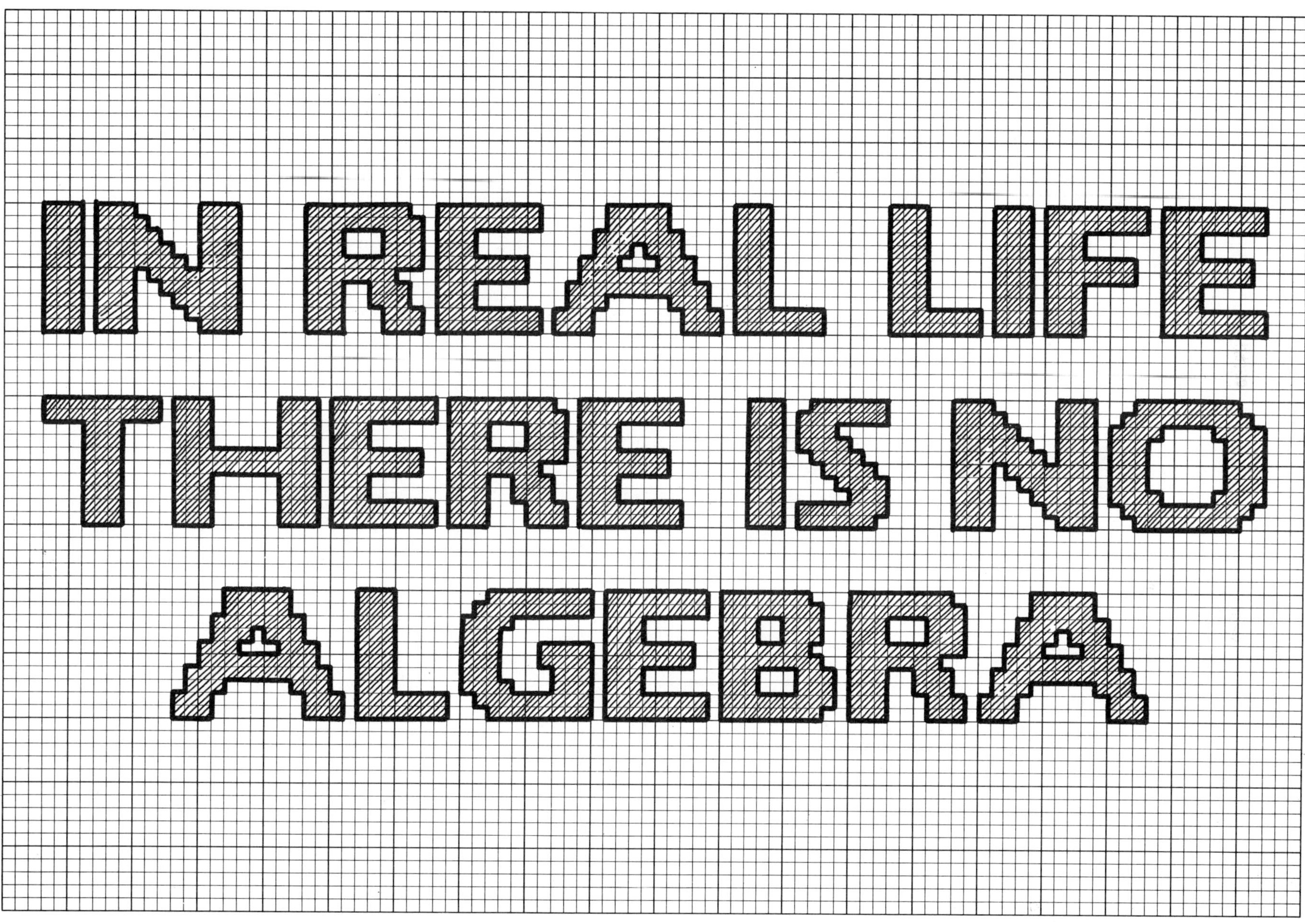
IN REAL LIFE
THERE IS NO
ALGEBRA

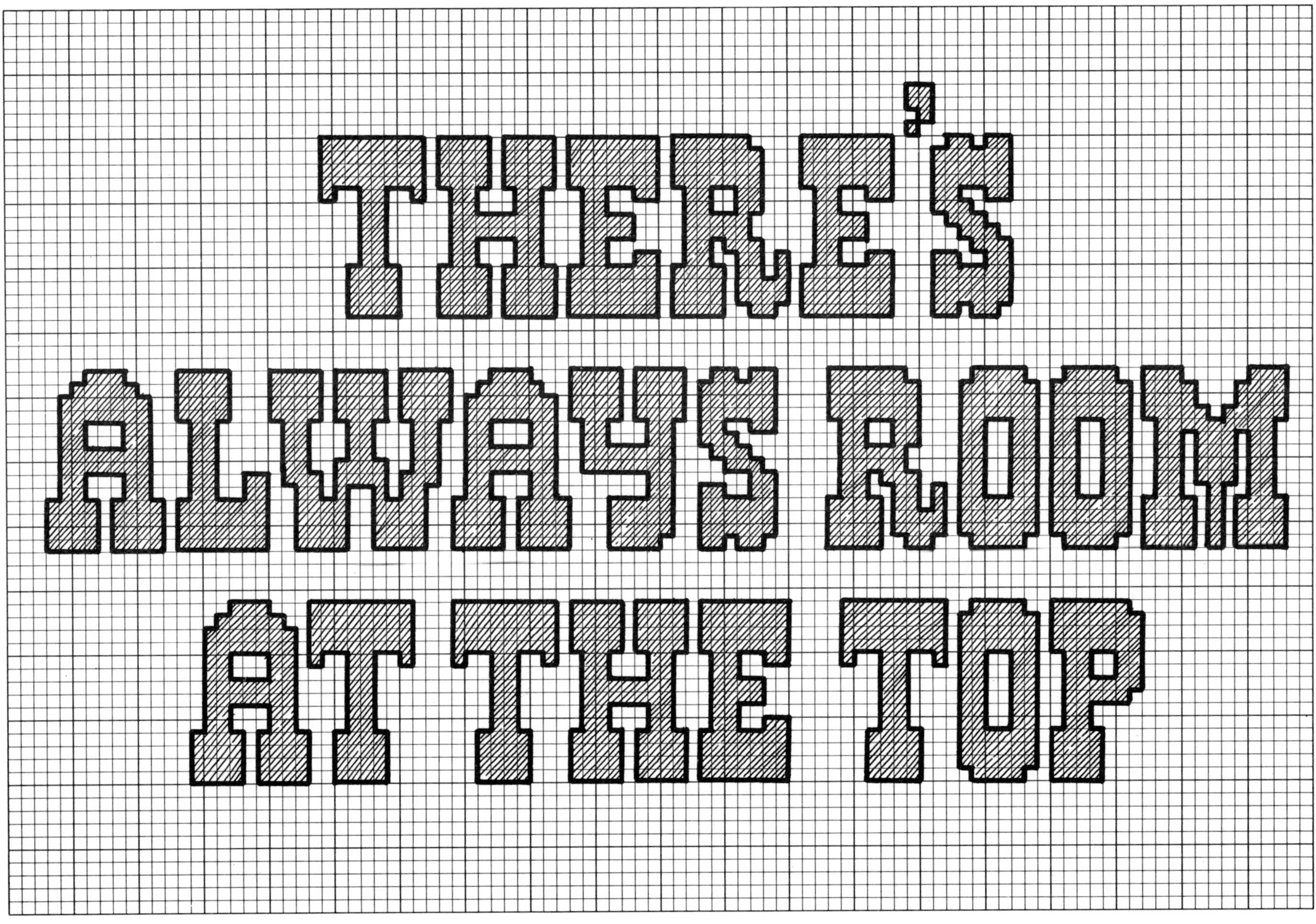
THERE'S
ALWAYS ROOM
AT THE TOP

AUNTIE EM,
HATE YOU-
HATE KANSAS-
TAKING THE DOG.
DOROTHY

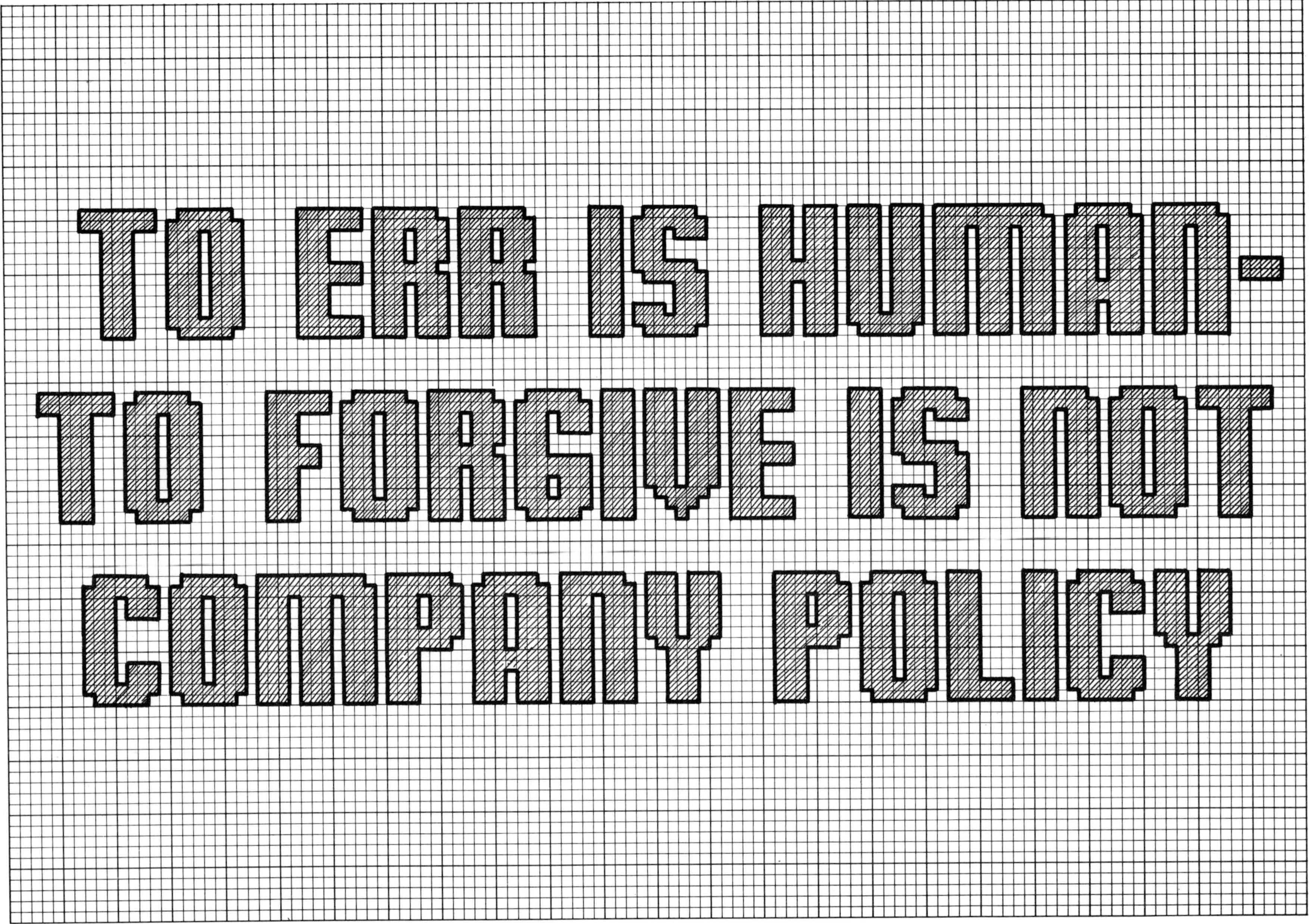
TO ERR IS HUMAN-
TO FORGIVE IS NOT
COMPANY POLICY

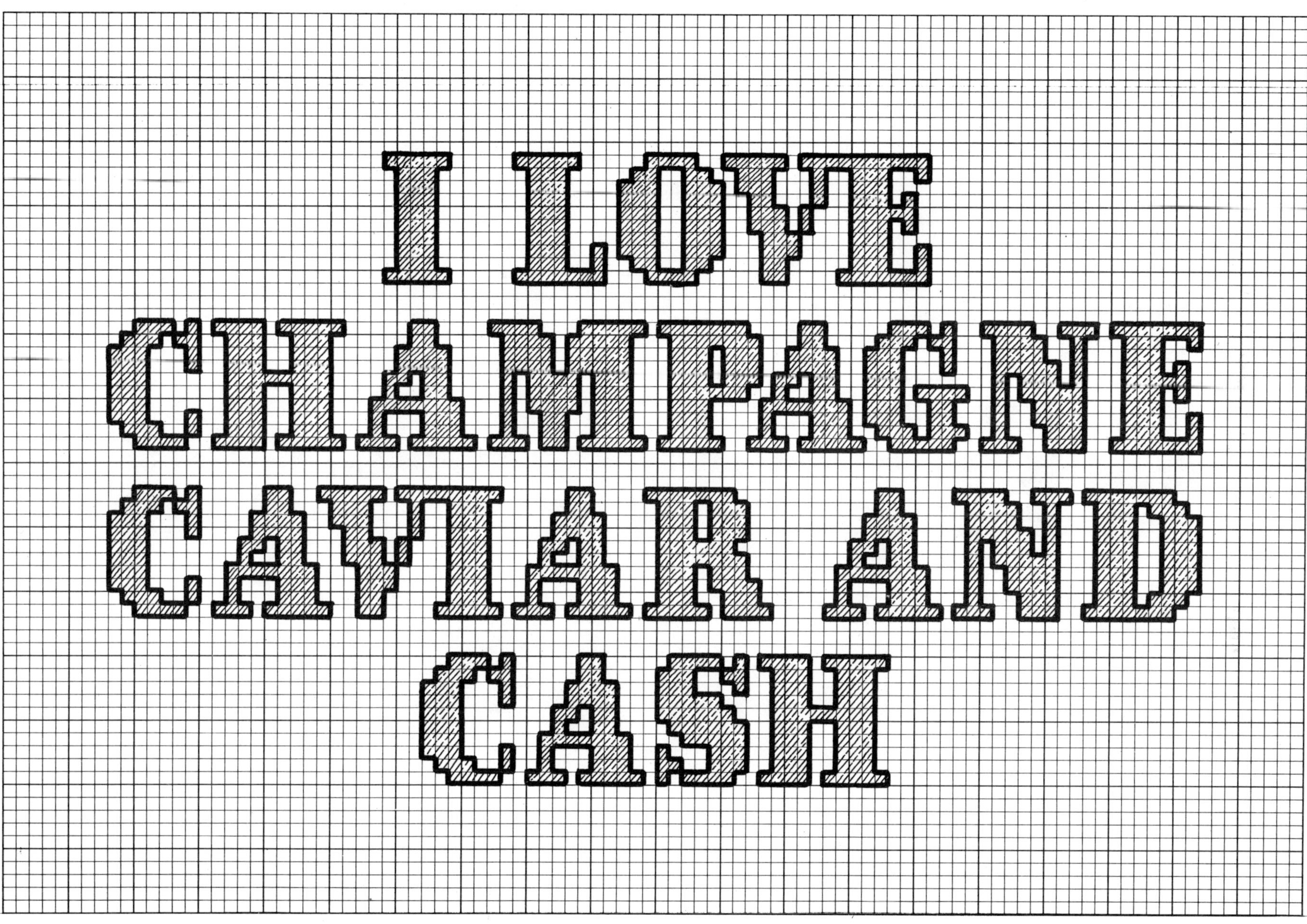
I LOVE
CHAMPAGNE
CAVIAR AND
CASH

GOD LOVES
WOMEN WITH
FAT THIGHS

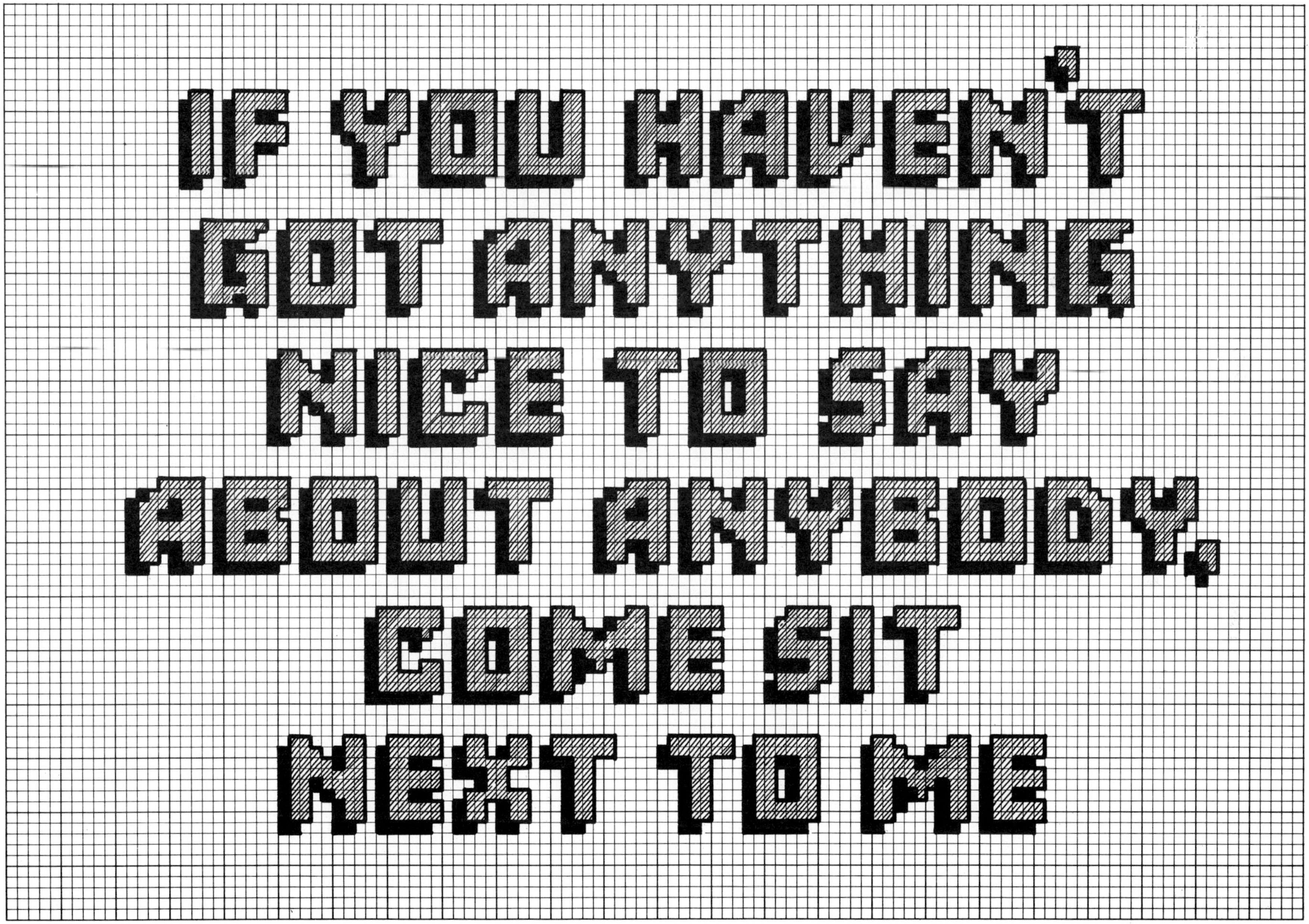

IF YOU HAVEN'T
GOT ANYTHING
NICE TO SAY
ABOUT ANYBODY,
COME SIT
NEXT TO ME

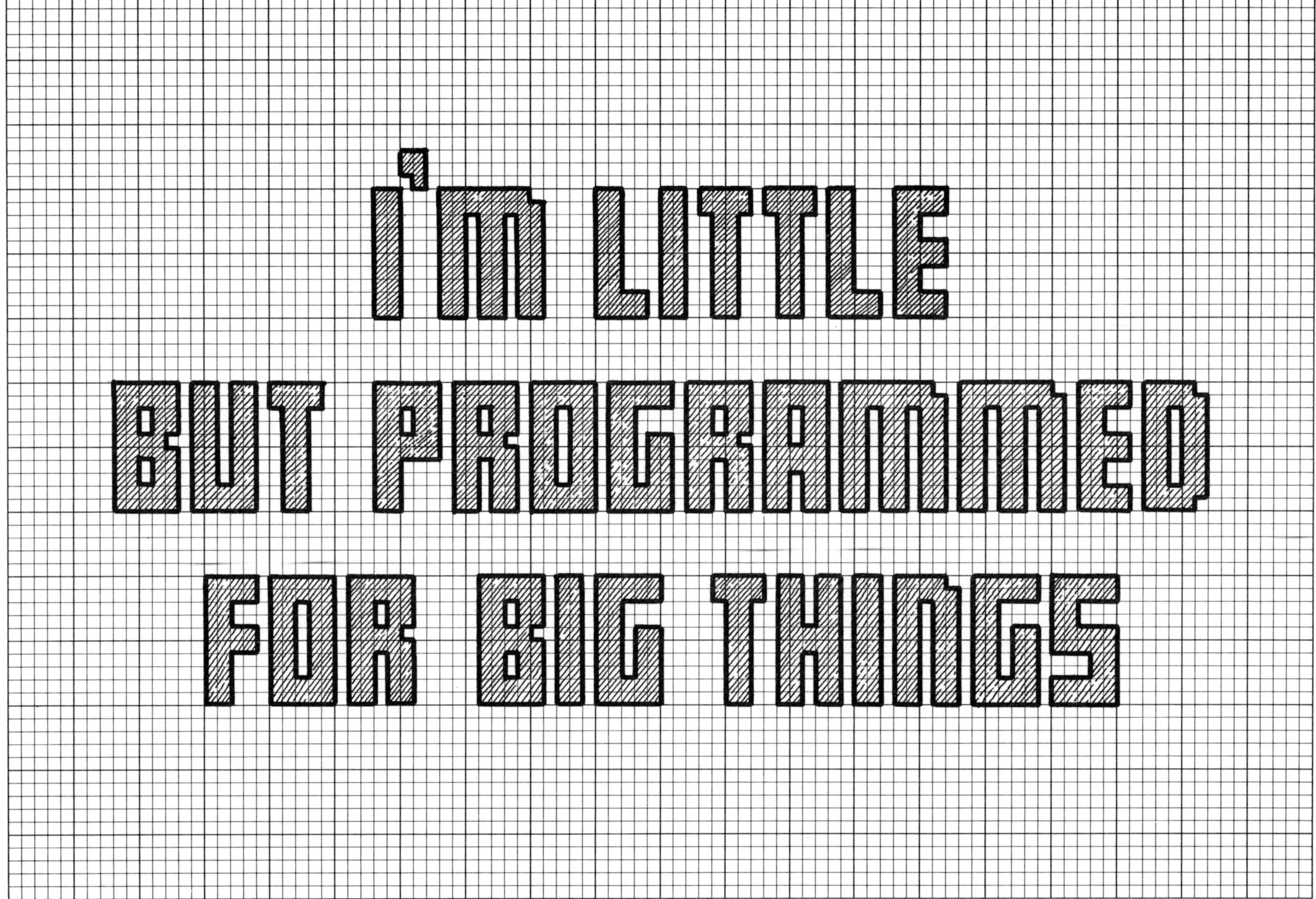
I'M LITTLE
BUT PROGRAMMED
FOR BIG THINGS

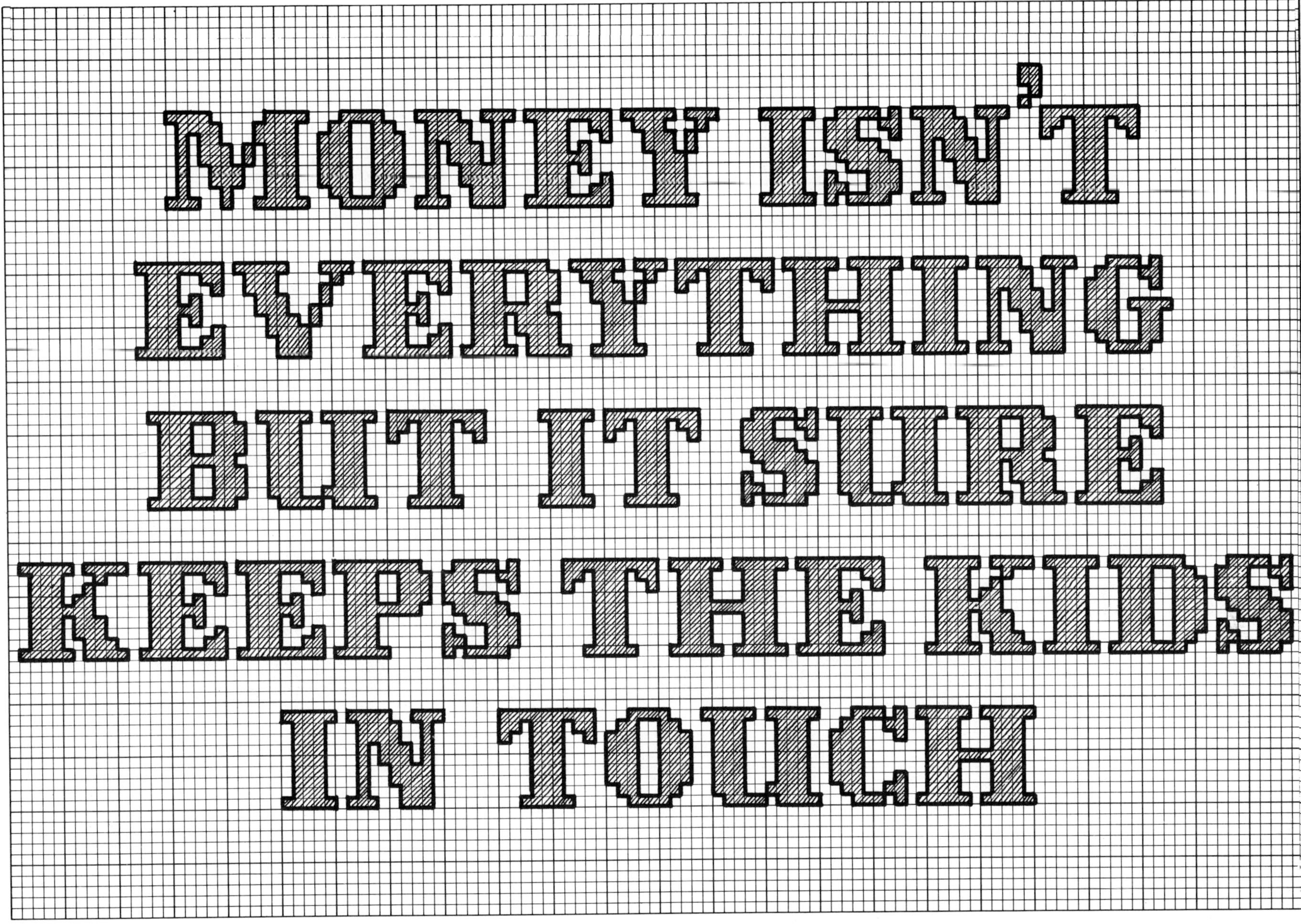
MONEY ISN'T
EVERYTHING
BUT IT SURE
KEEPS THE KIDS
IN TOUCH

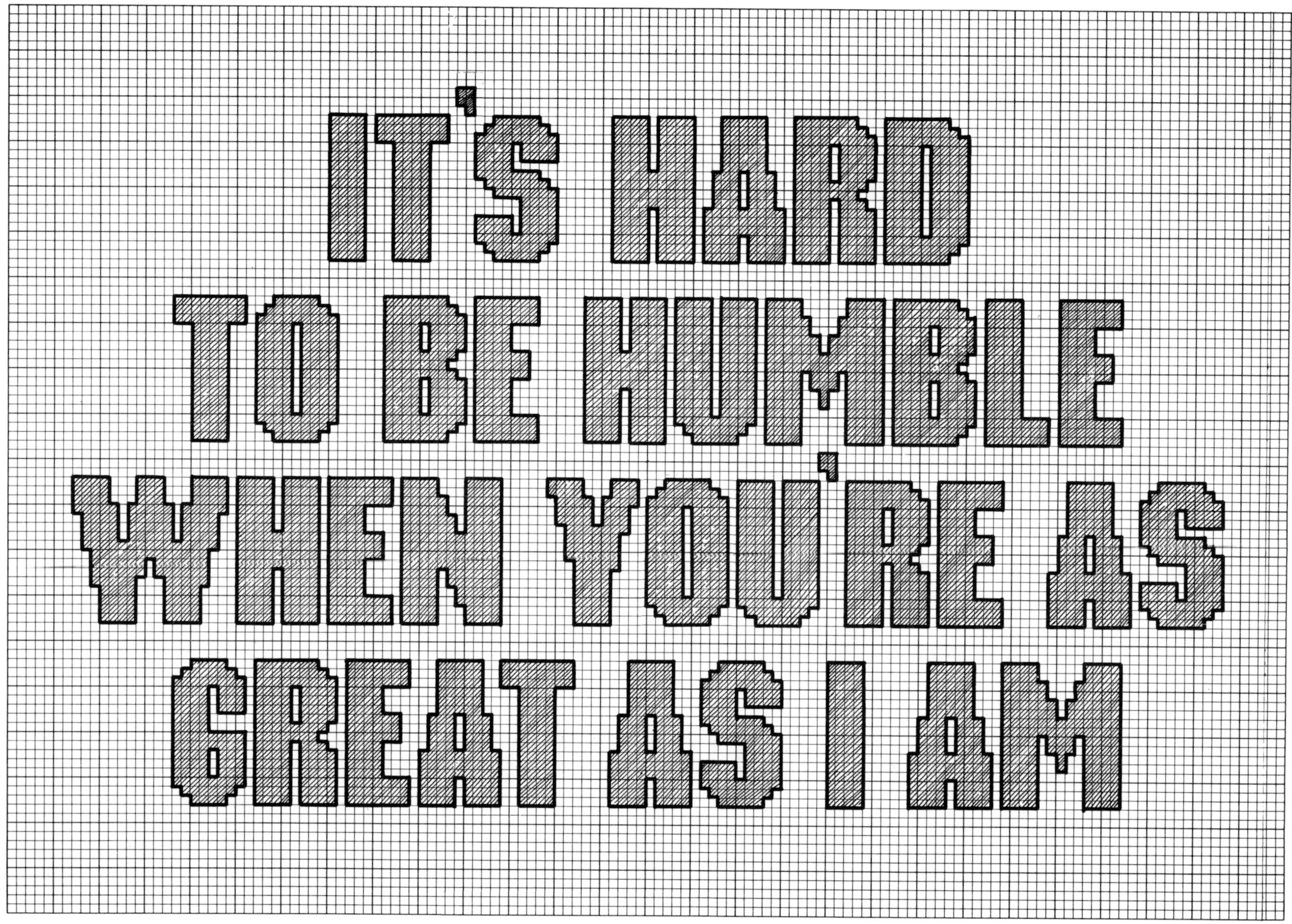
IT'S HARD
TO BE HUMBLE
WHEN YOU'RE AS
GREAT AS I AM

BUY
SHEEP
SELL
DEER

IF YOU
MUST SMOKE,
PLEASE DON'T
EXHALE

DON'T BLOW IT-
GOOD PLANETS
ARE HARD
TO FIND

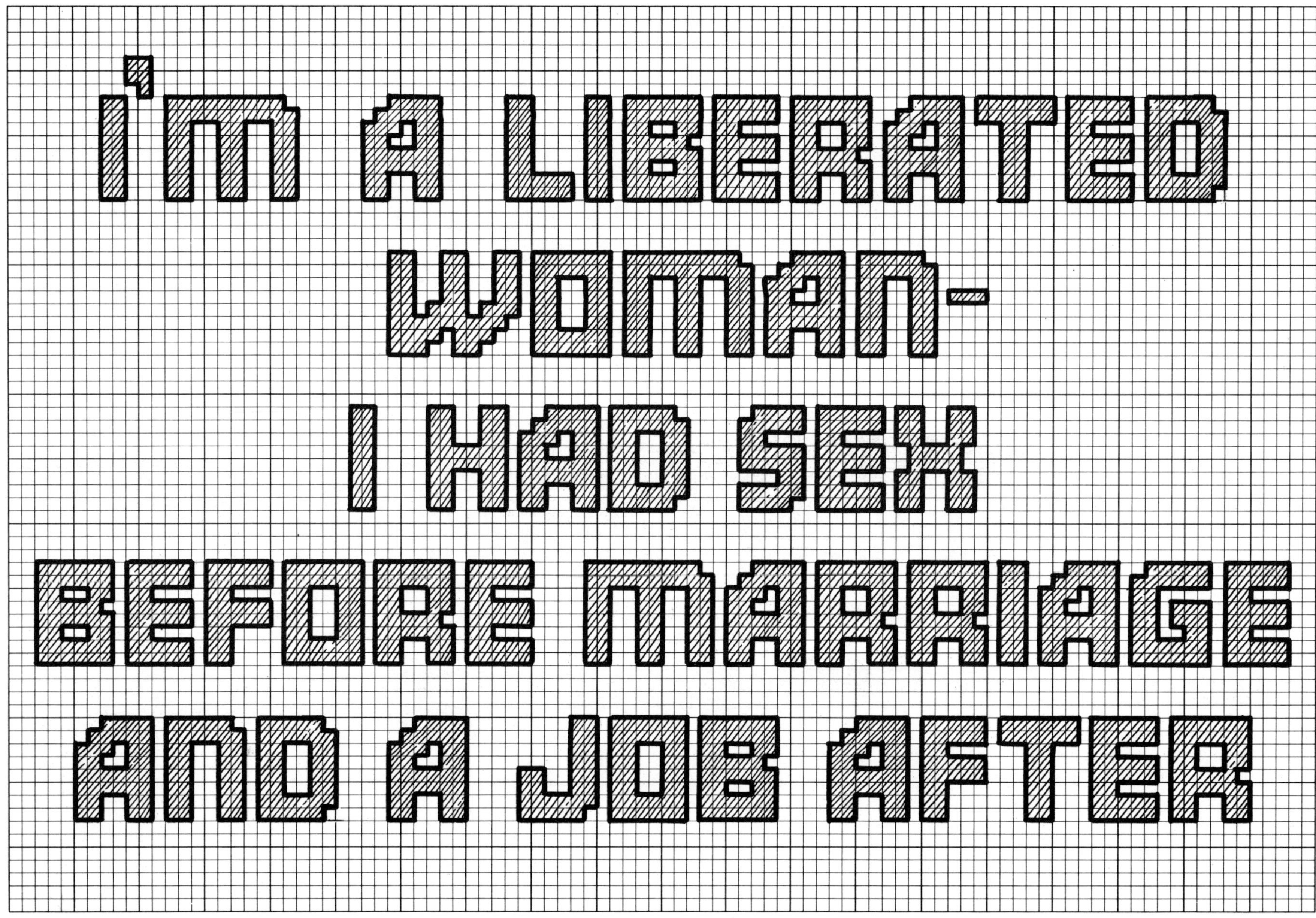
I'M A LIBERATED
WOMAN-
I HAD SEX
BEFORE MARRIAGE
AND A JOB AFTER

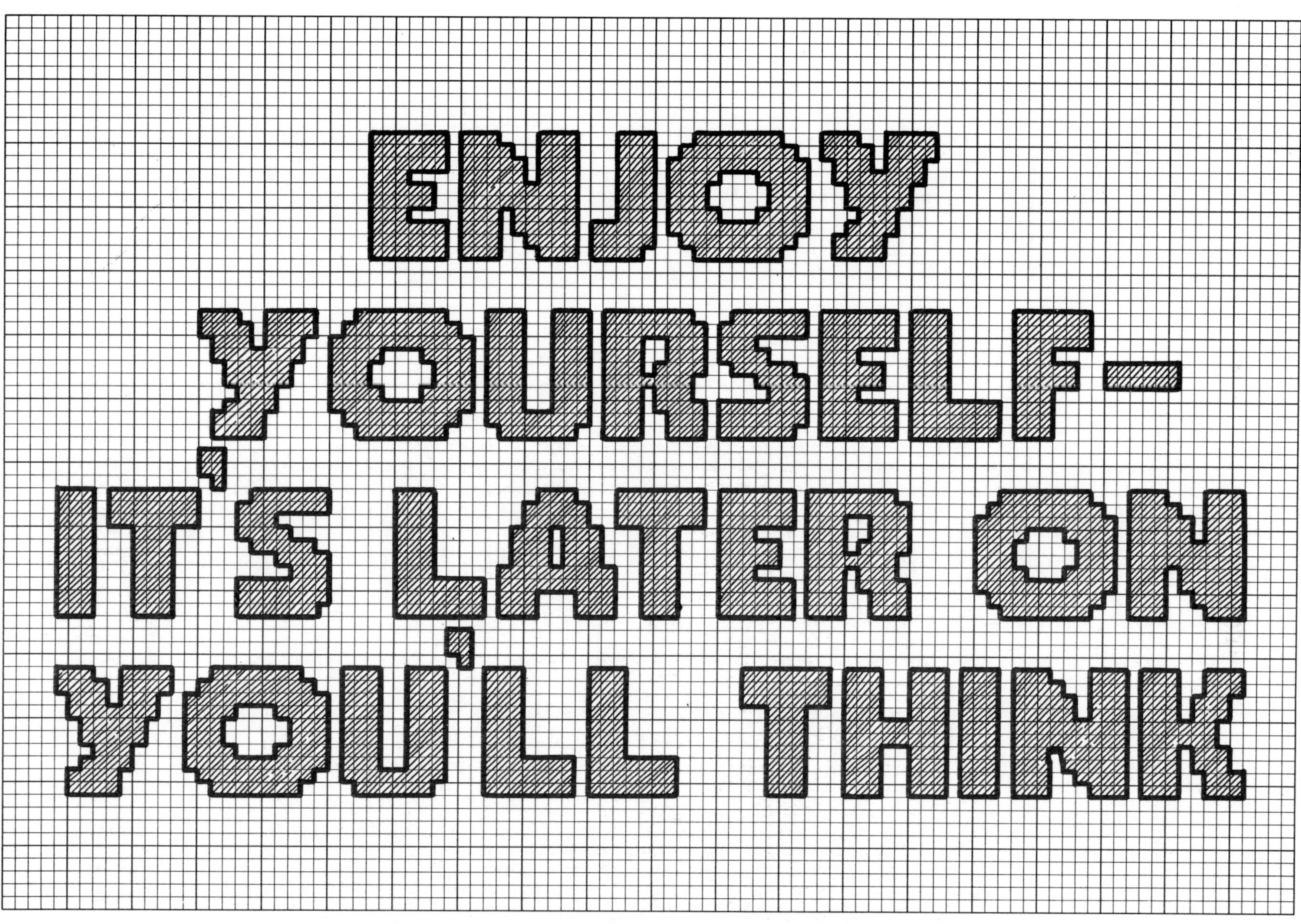
ENJOY
YOURSELF-
IT'S LATER ON
YOU'LL THINK

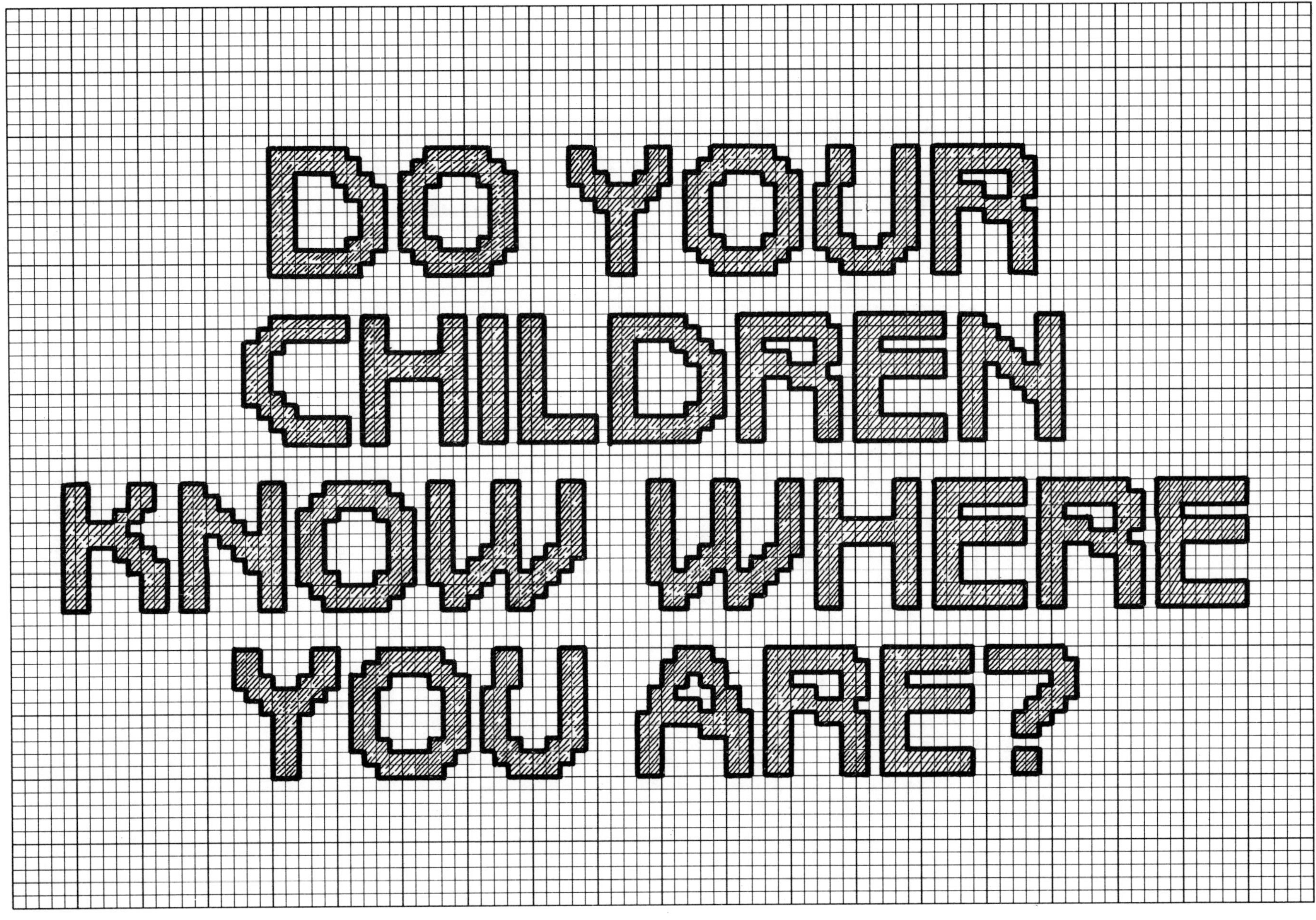
DO YOUR
CHILDREN
KNOW WHERE
YOU ARE?

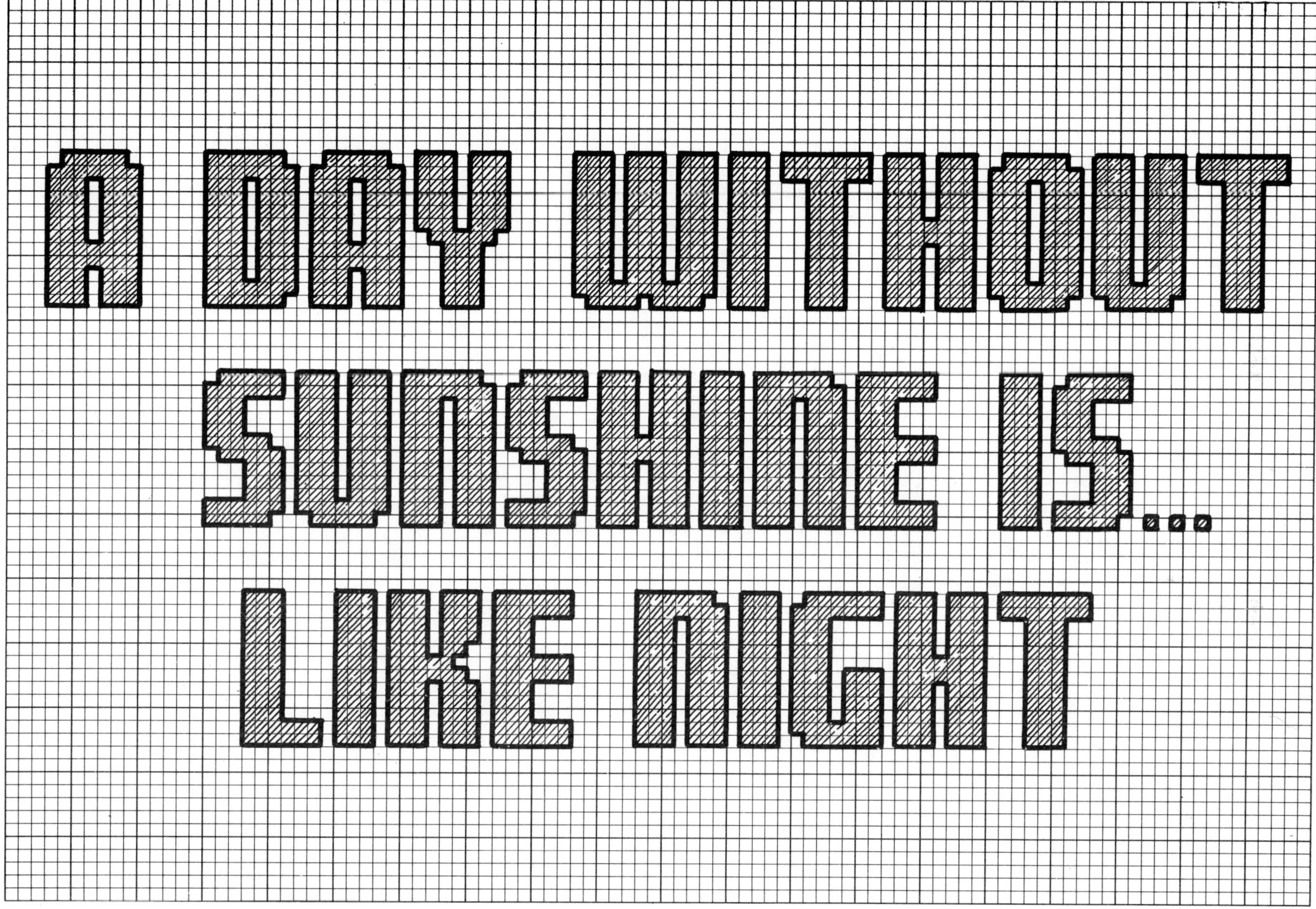
A DAY WITHOUT
SUNSHINE IS...
LIKE NIGHT

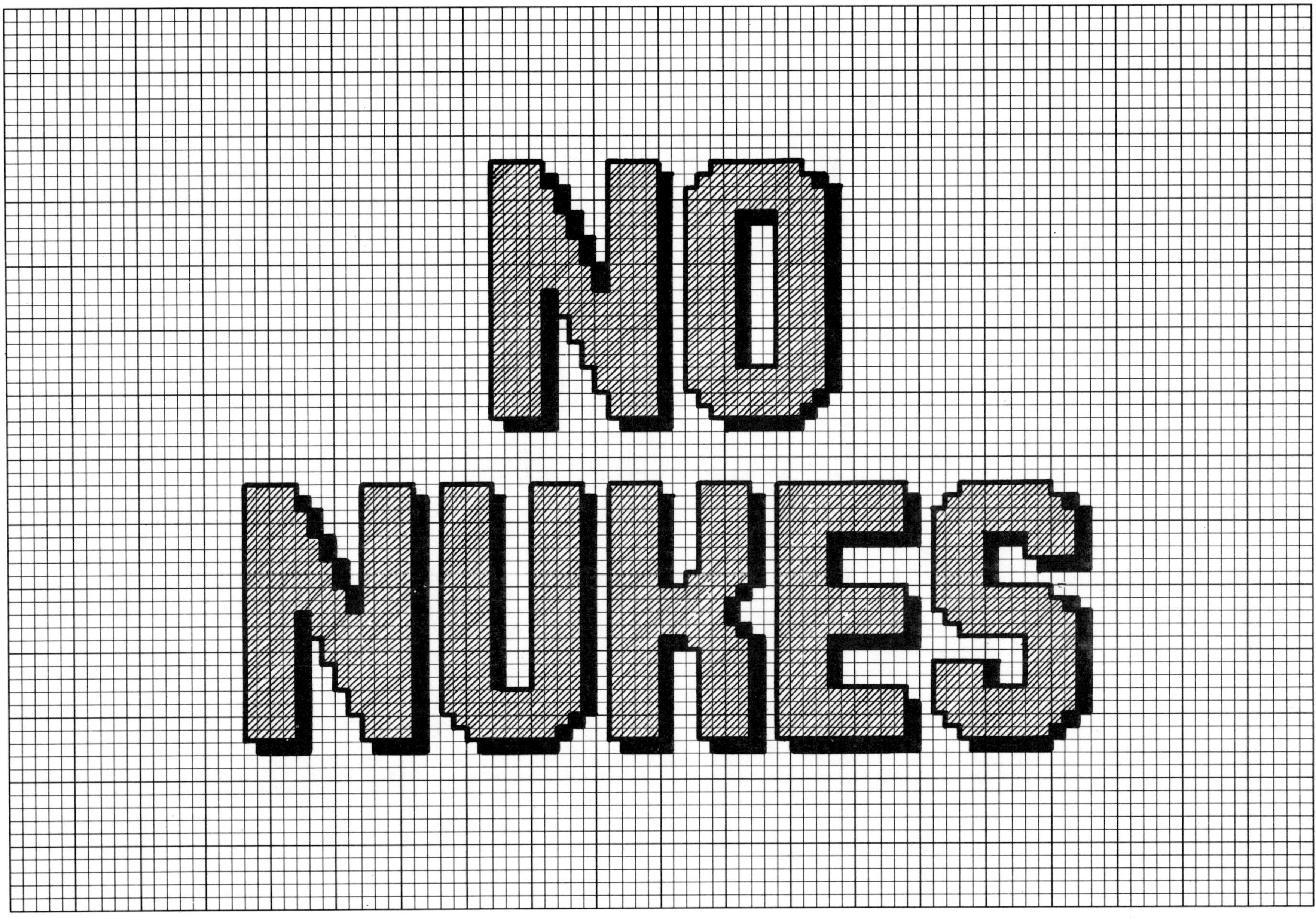
NO
NUKES

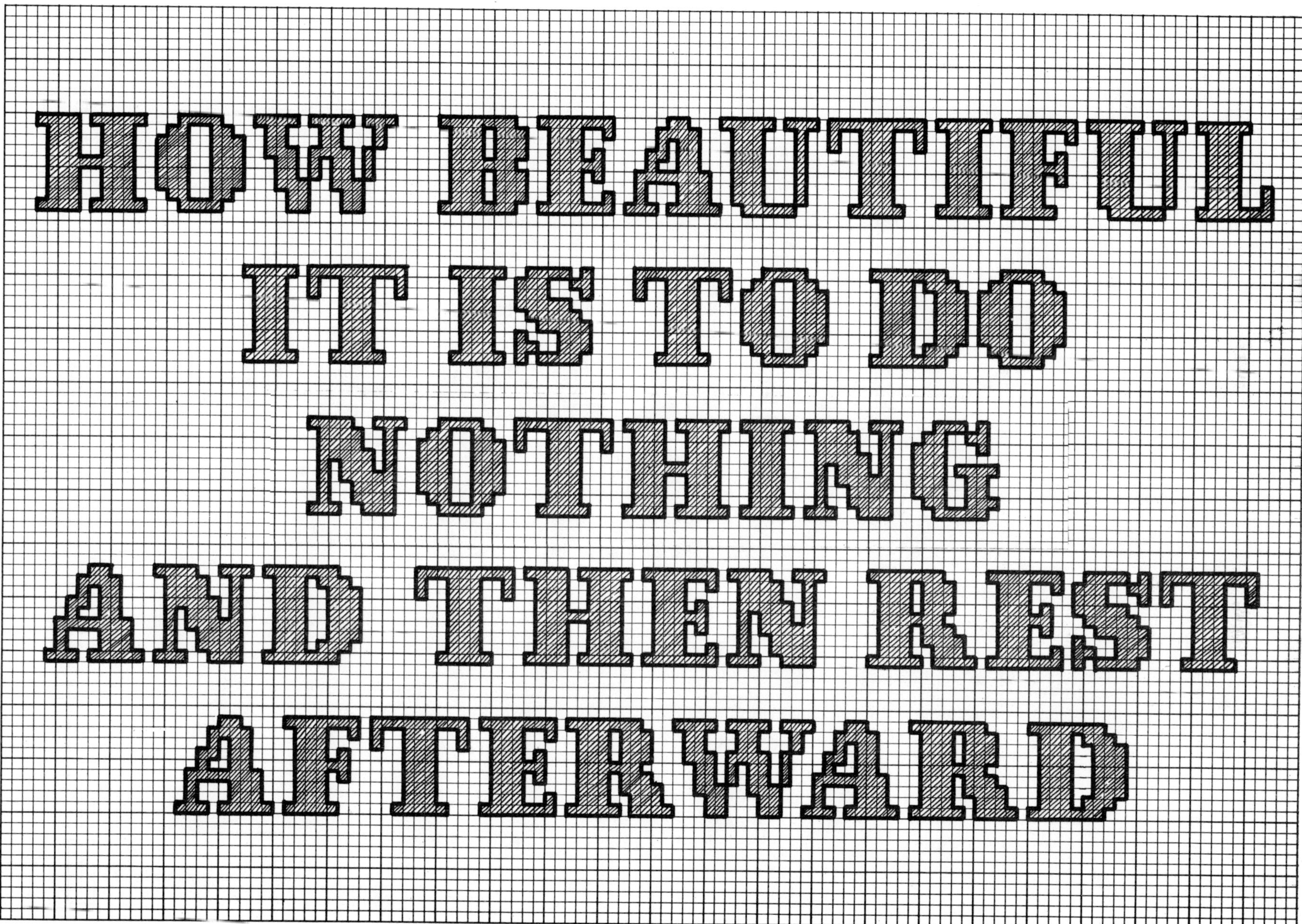
HOW BEAUTIFUL
IT IS TO DO
NOTHING
AND THEN REST
AFTERWARD

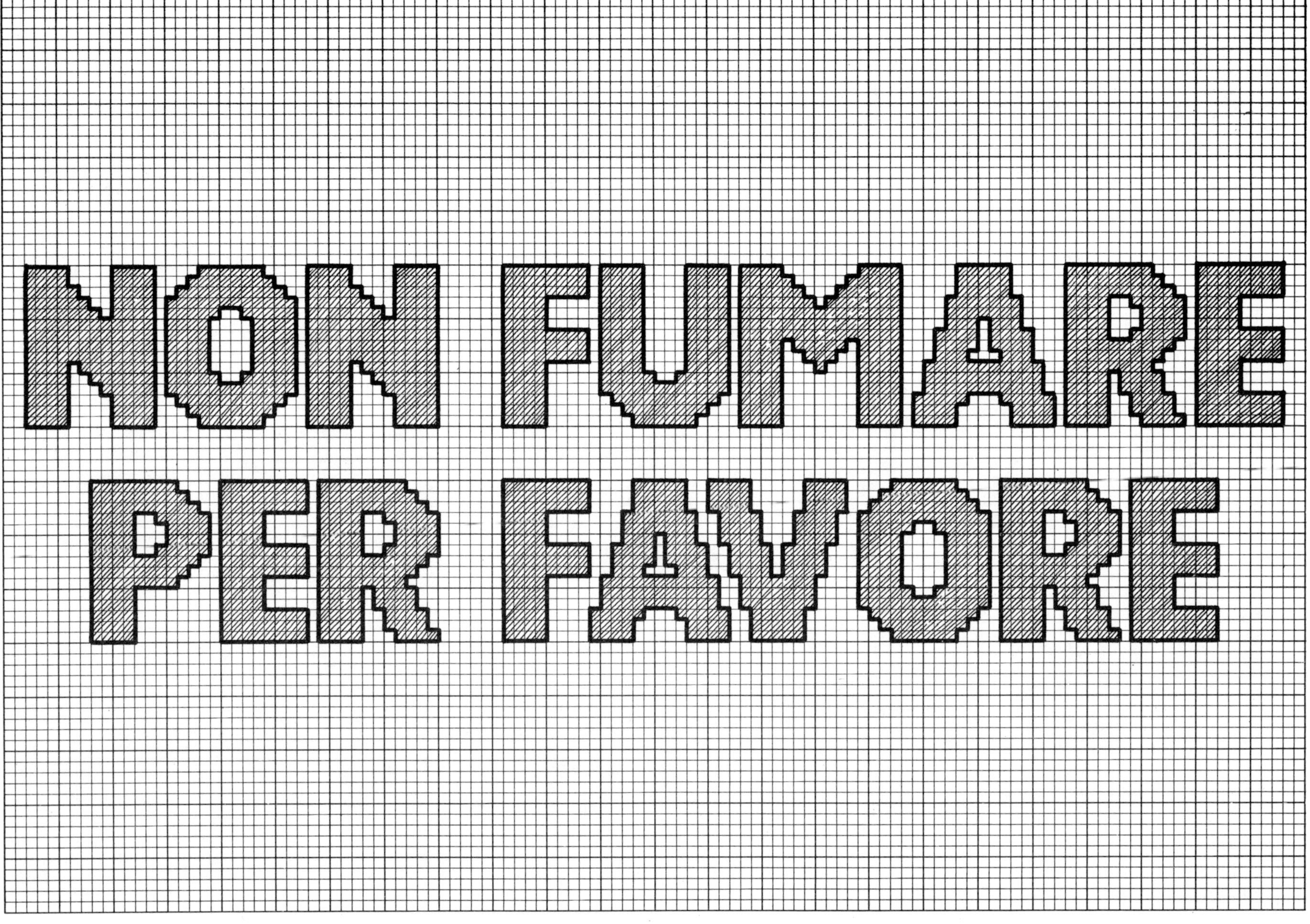
NON FUMARE
PER FAVORE

TOTO...
I HAVE A FEELING
WE'RE NOT IN
KANSAS ANYMORE

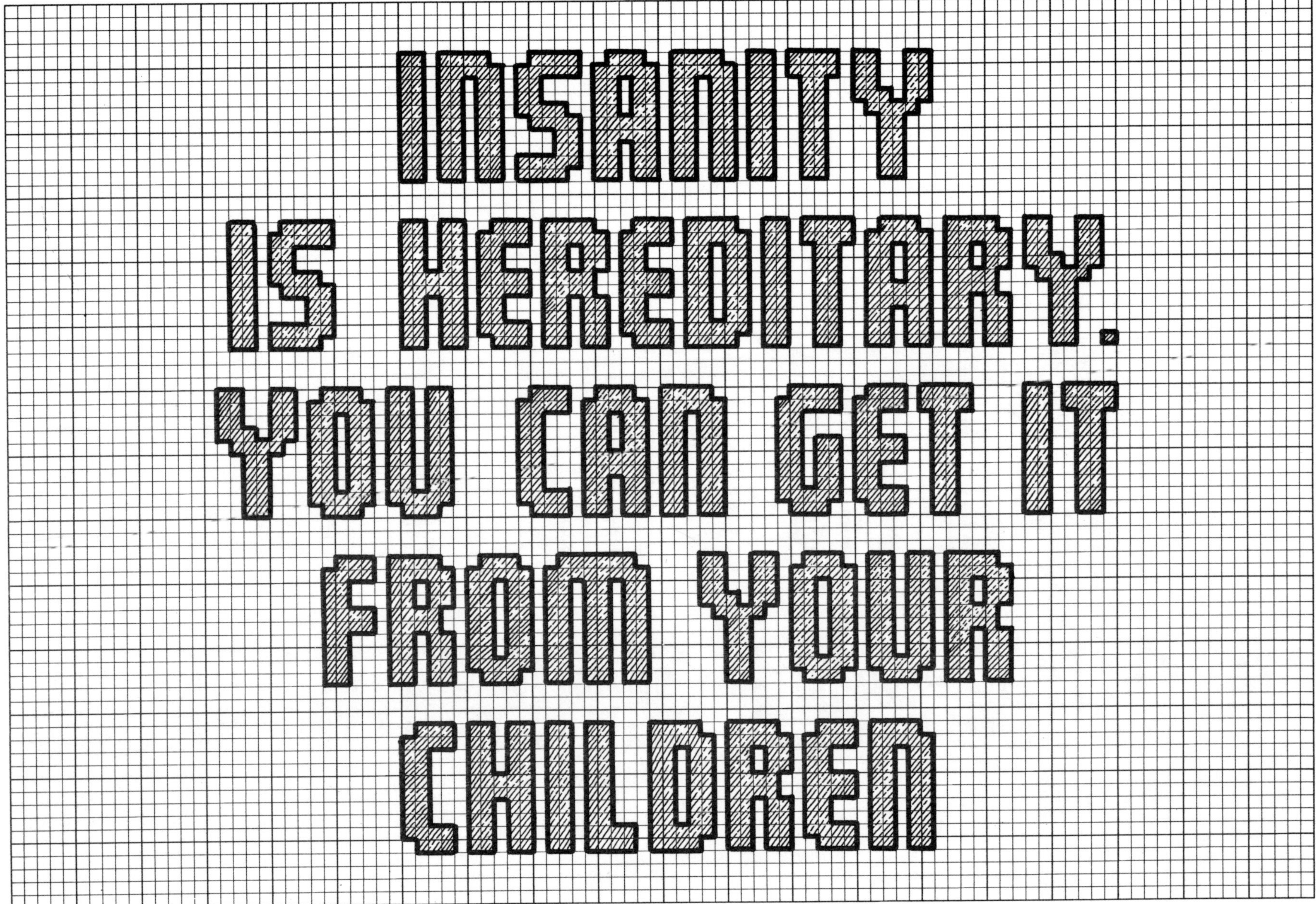
INSANITY
IS HEREDITARY.
YOU CAN GET IT
FROM YOUR
CHILDREN

TOO MUCH OF
A GOOD THING
IS WONDERFUL

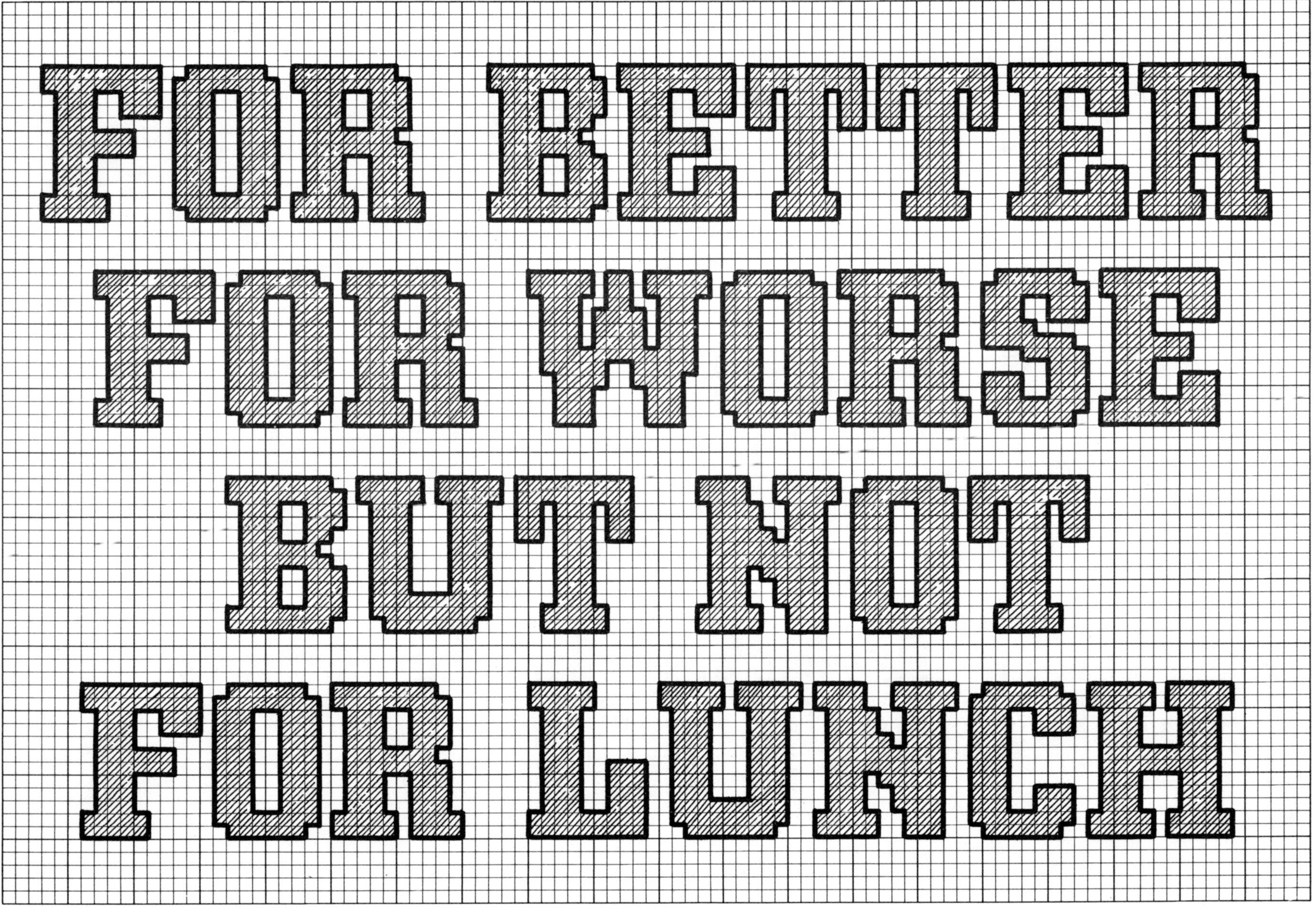
FOR BETTER
FOR WORSE
BUT NOT
FOR LUNCH

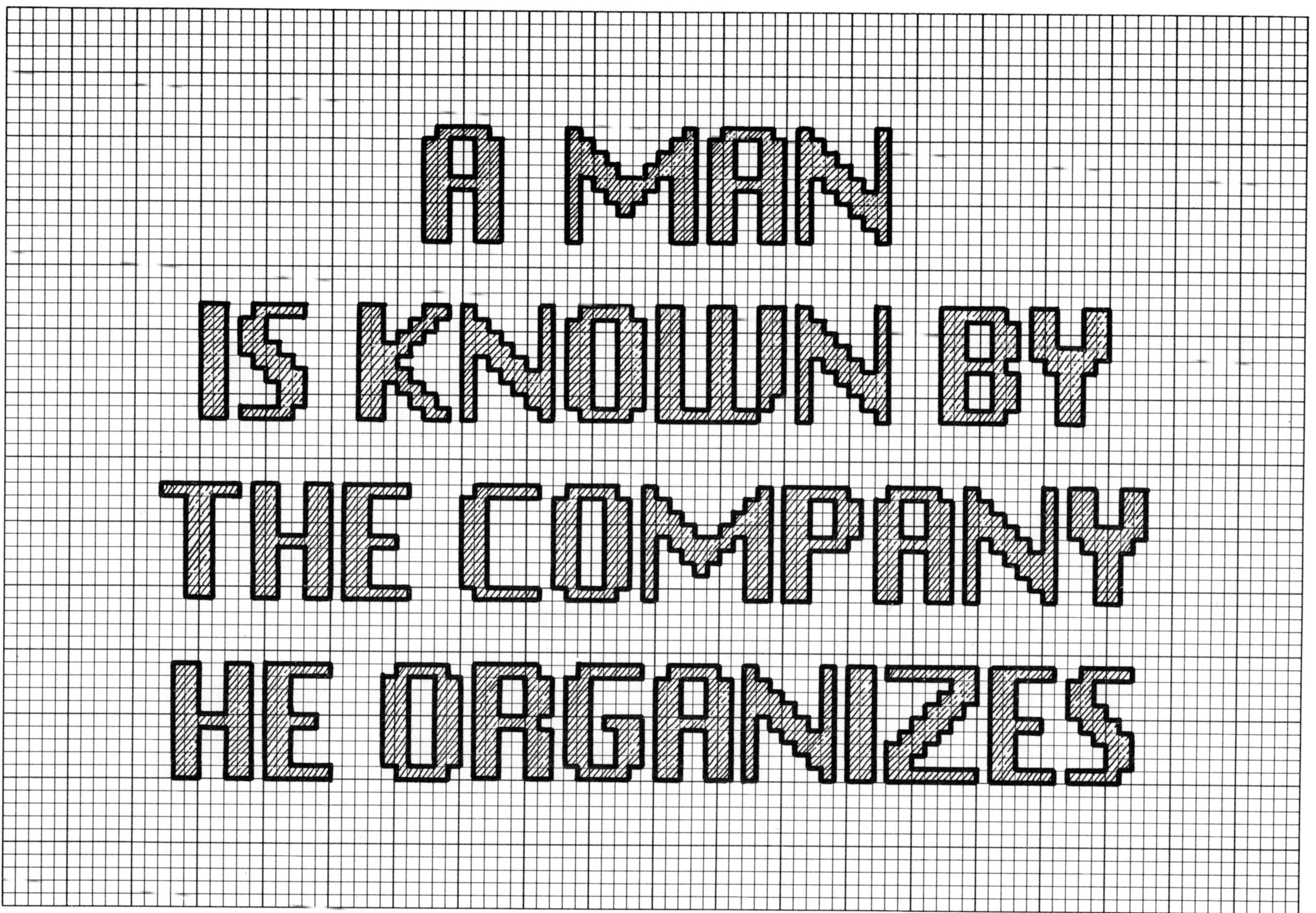
A MAN
IS KNOWN BY
THE COMPANY
HE ORGANIZES

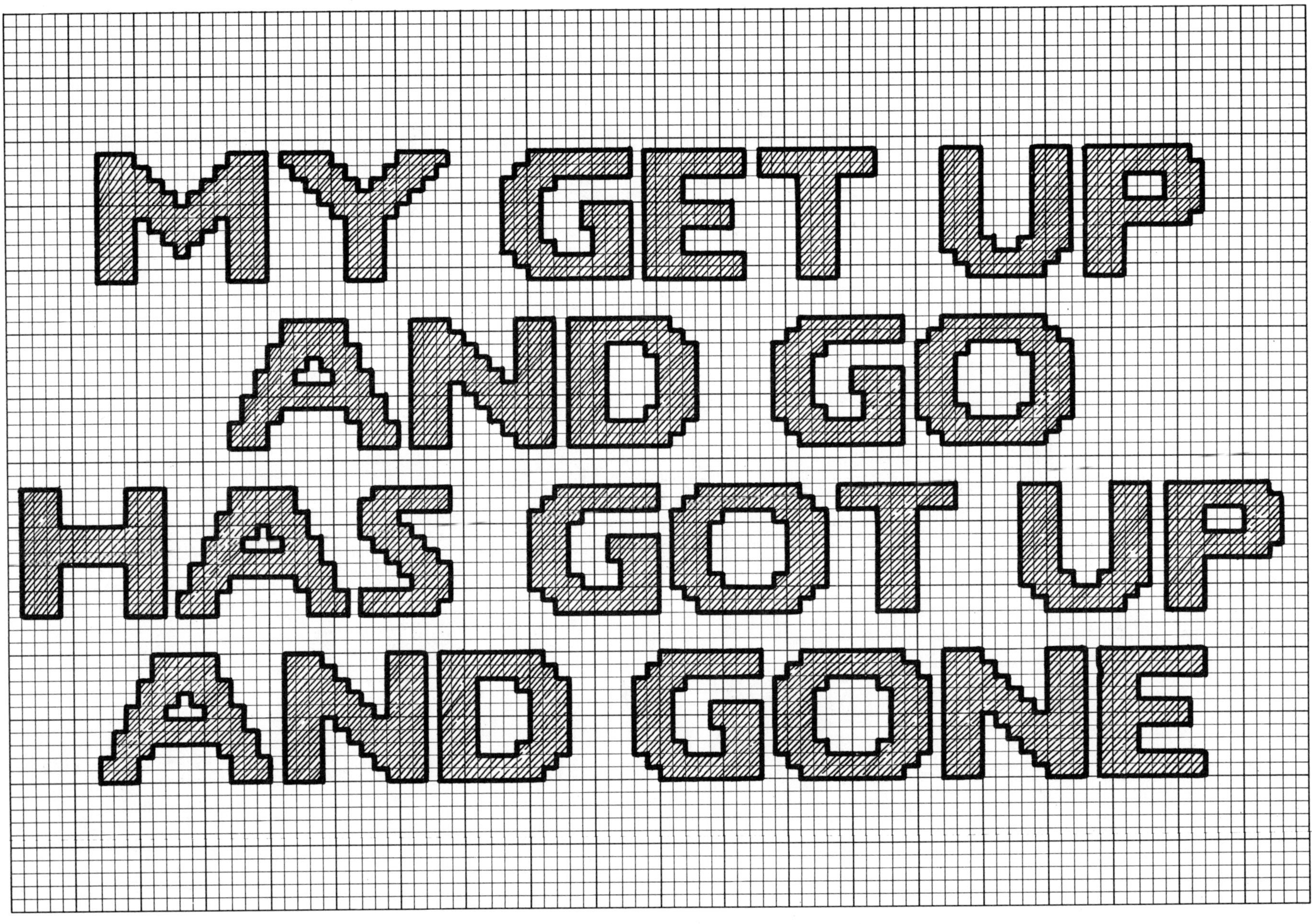
MY GET UP
AND GO
HAS GOT UP
AND GONE

THANK YOU
FOR NOT
WHIMPERING

YOU'RE
24
KARAT

YOU'LL NEVER
KNOW HOW MANY
FRIENDS YOU HAVE
TILL YOU GET
A SUMMER PLACE

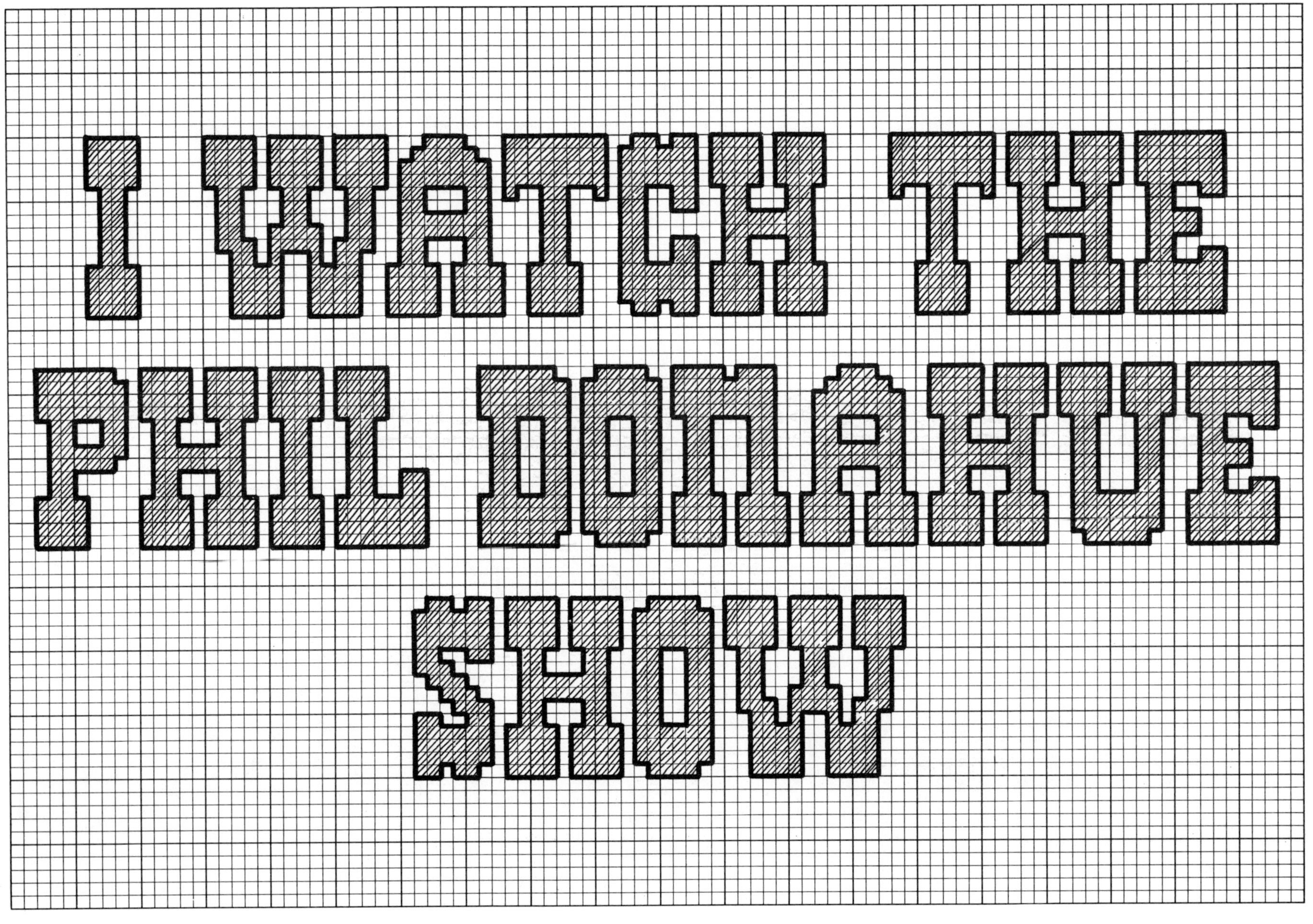
I WATCH THE
PHIL DONAHUE
SHOW

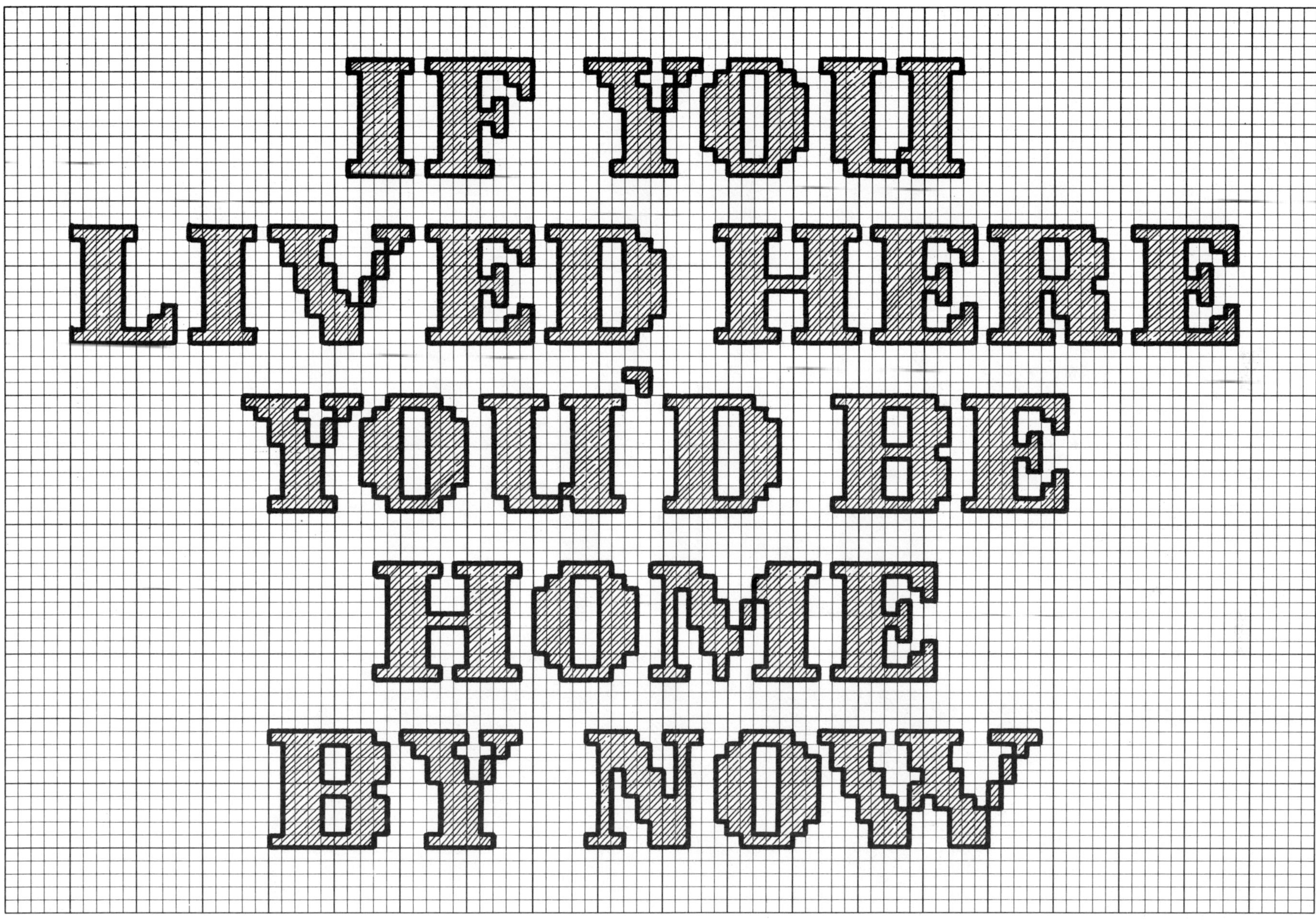
IF YOU
LIVED HERE
YOU'D BE
HOME
BY NOW

BE
REASONABLE,
DO IT
MY WAY

WE'RE LIVING
HAPPILY
EVER AFTER
ON A DAY-TO-DAY
BASIS

MORAL
VICTORIES
DON'T COUNT

THE BEST
THINGS IN LIFE
ARE CHOCOLATE

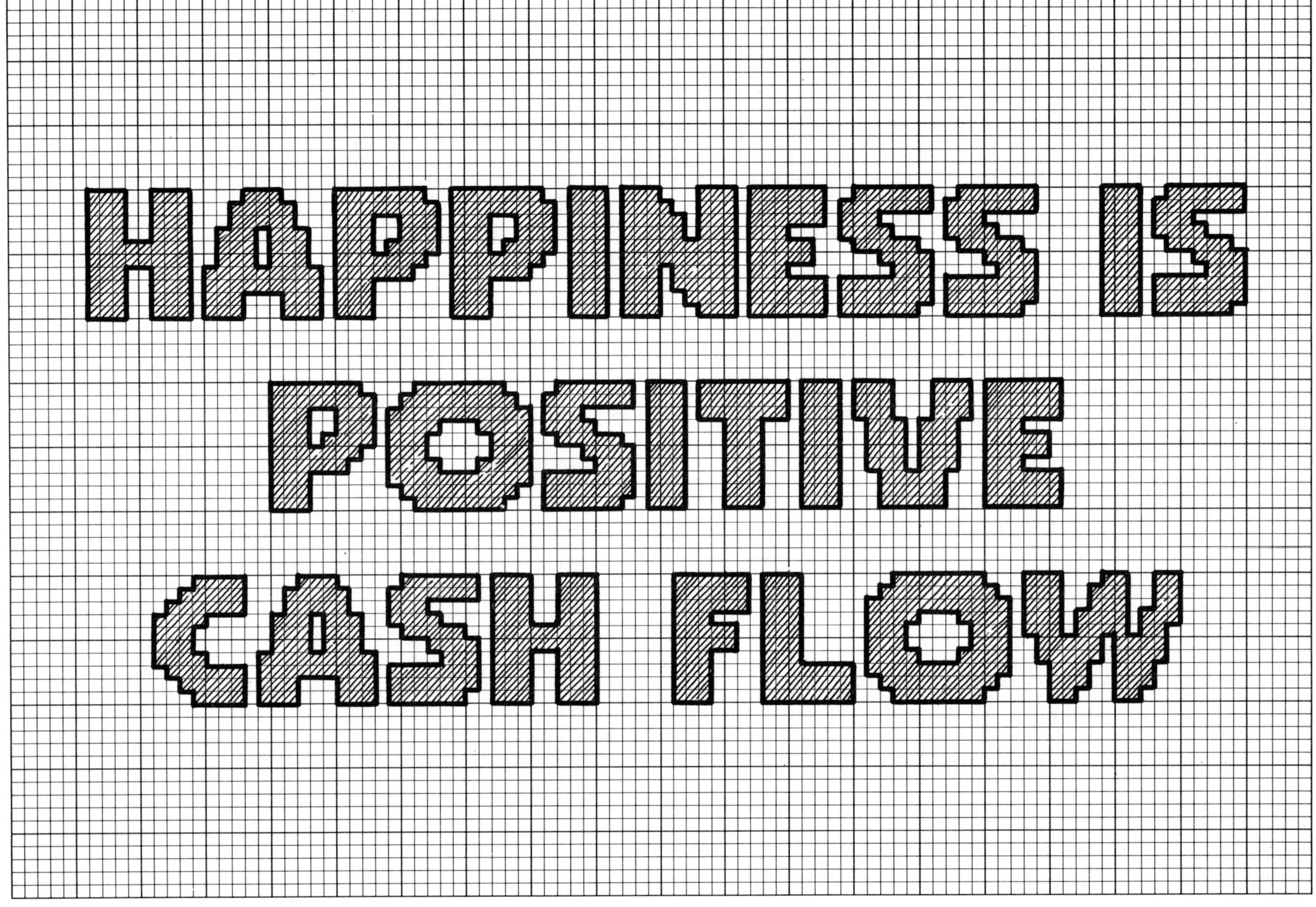
HAPPINESS IS
POSITIVE
CASH FLOW

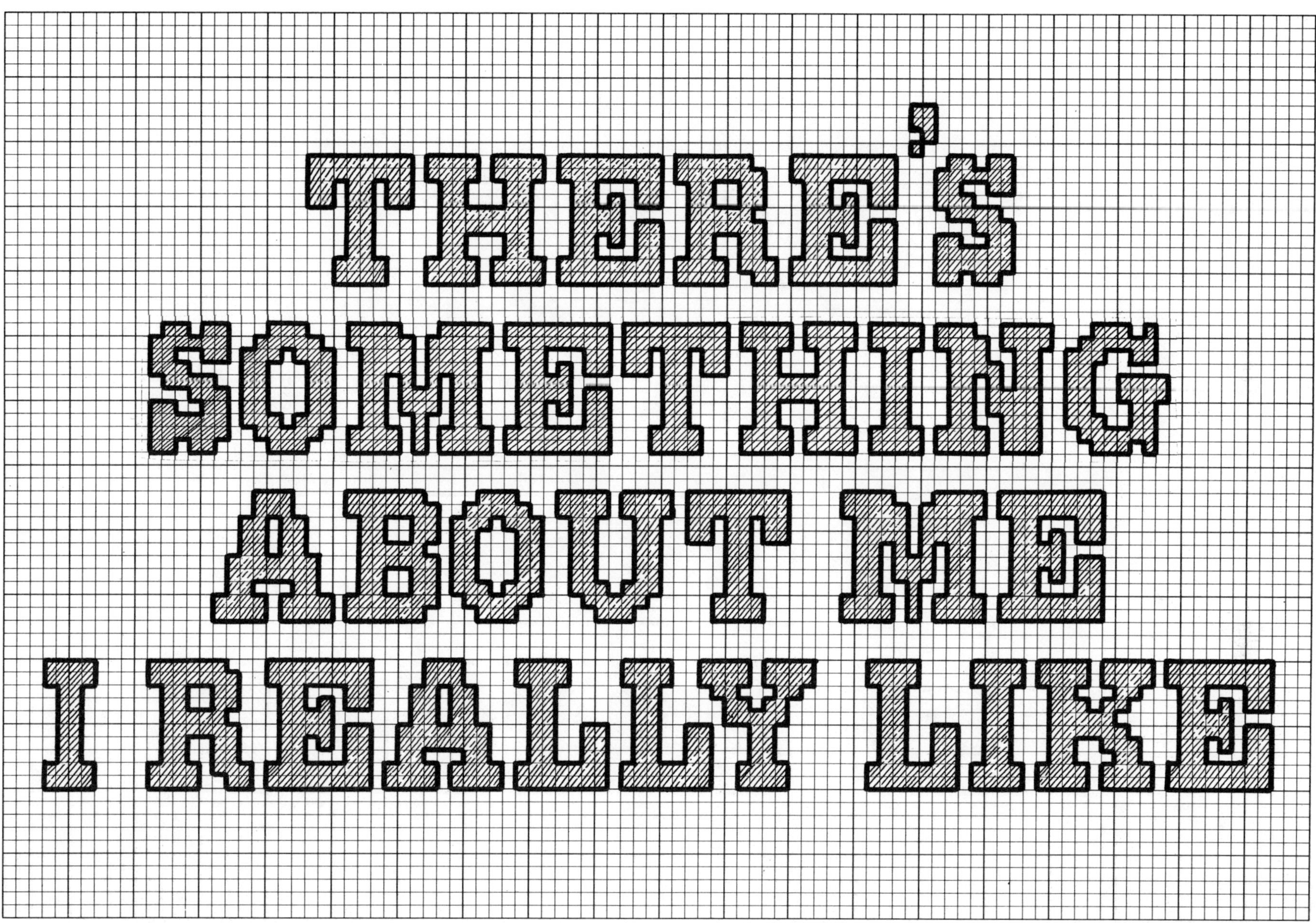
THERE'S
SOMETHING
ABOUT ME
I REALLY LIKE

LOVE
THY NEIGHBOR
BUT DON'T
GET CAUGHT

WHEN THE GOING
GETS TOUGH
THE TOUGH
GO SHOPPING

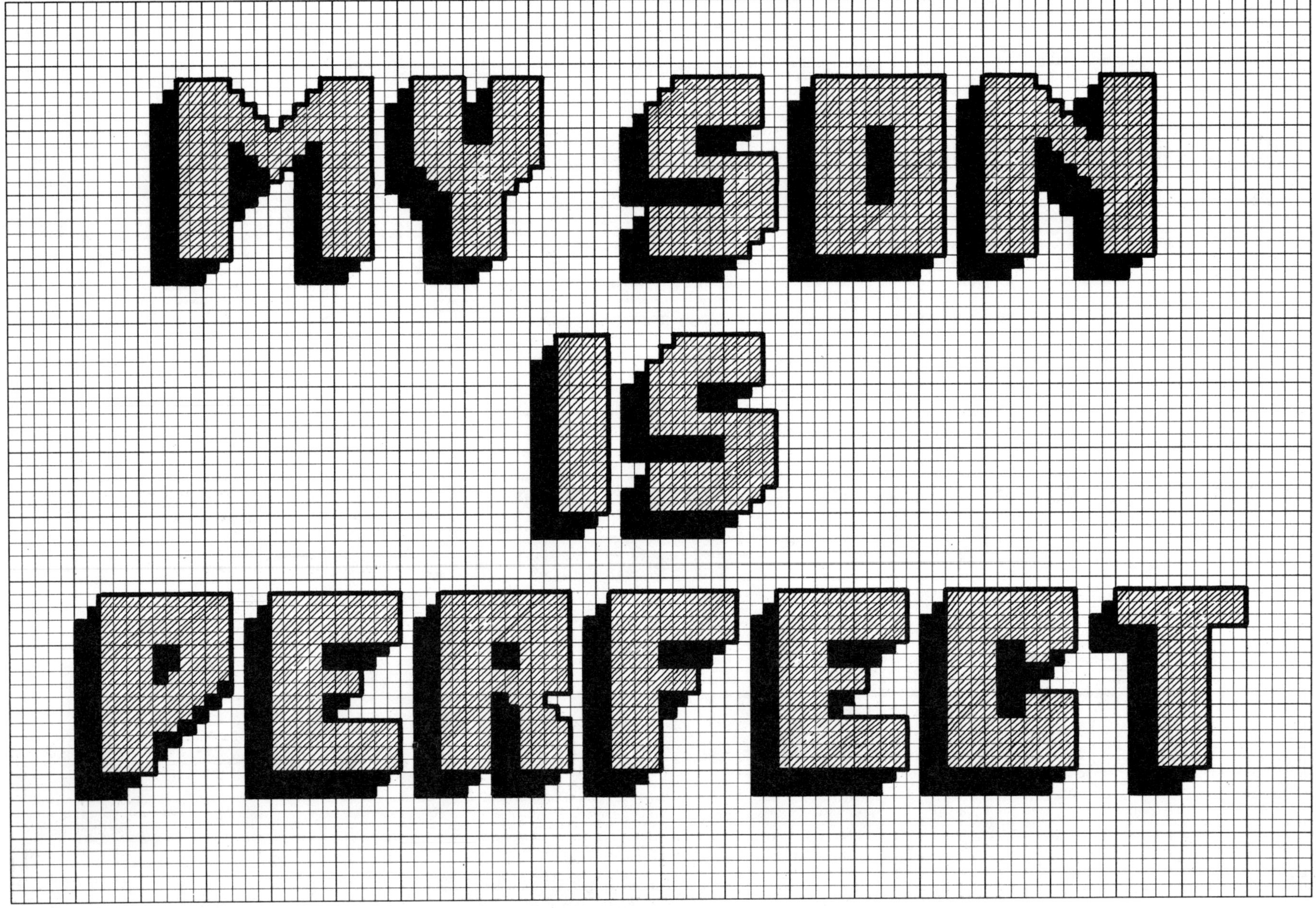
MY SON
IS
PERFECT

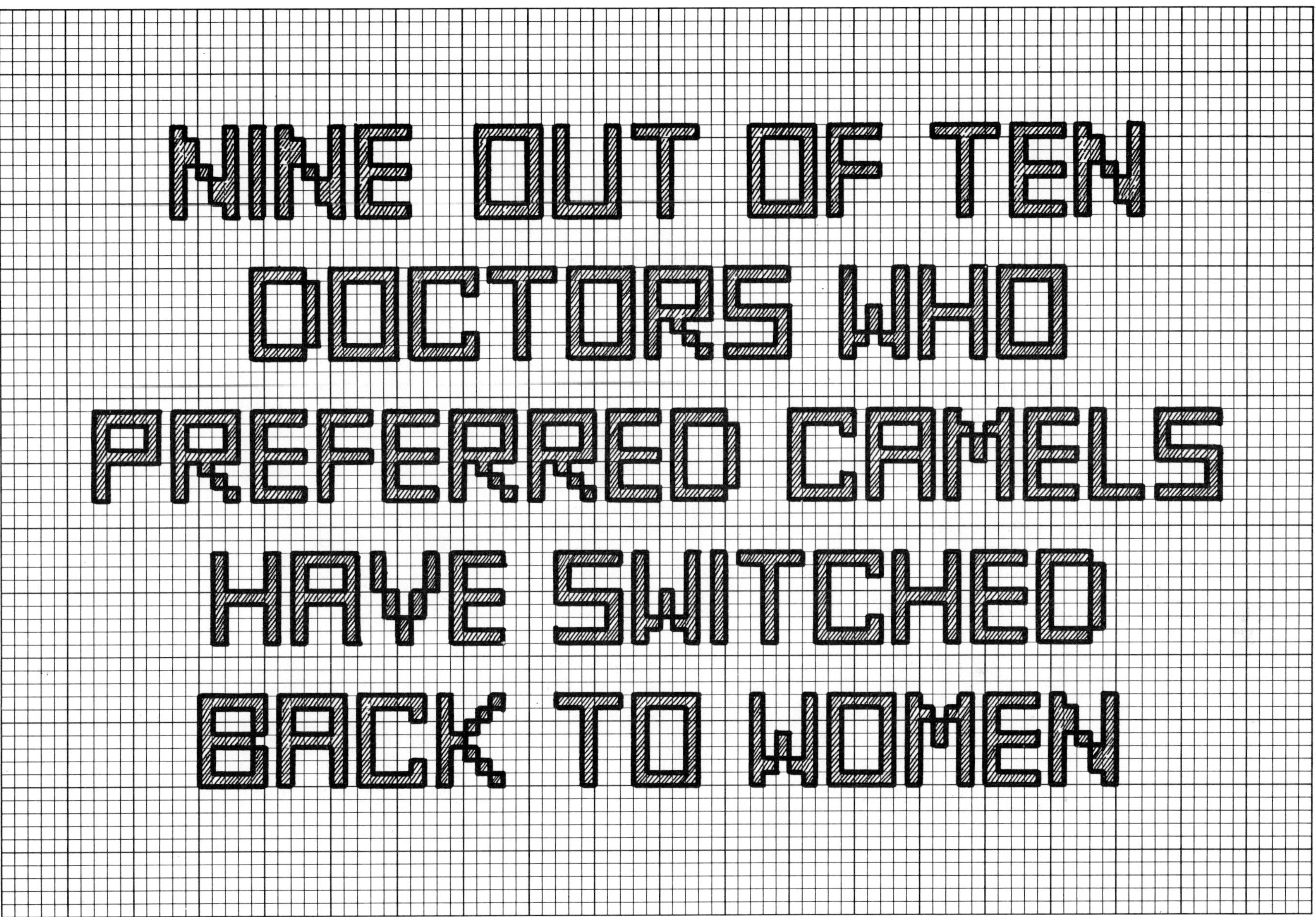
NINE OUT OF TEN
DOCTORS WHO
PREFERRED CAMELS
HAVE SWITCHED
BACK TO WOMEN

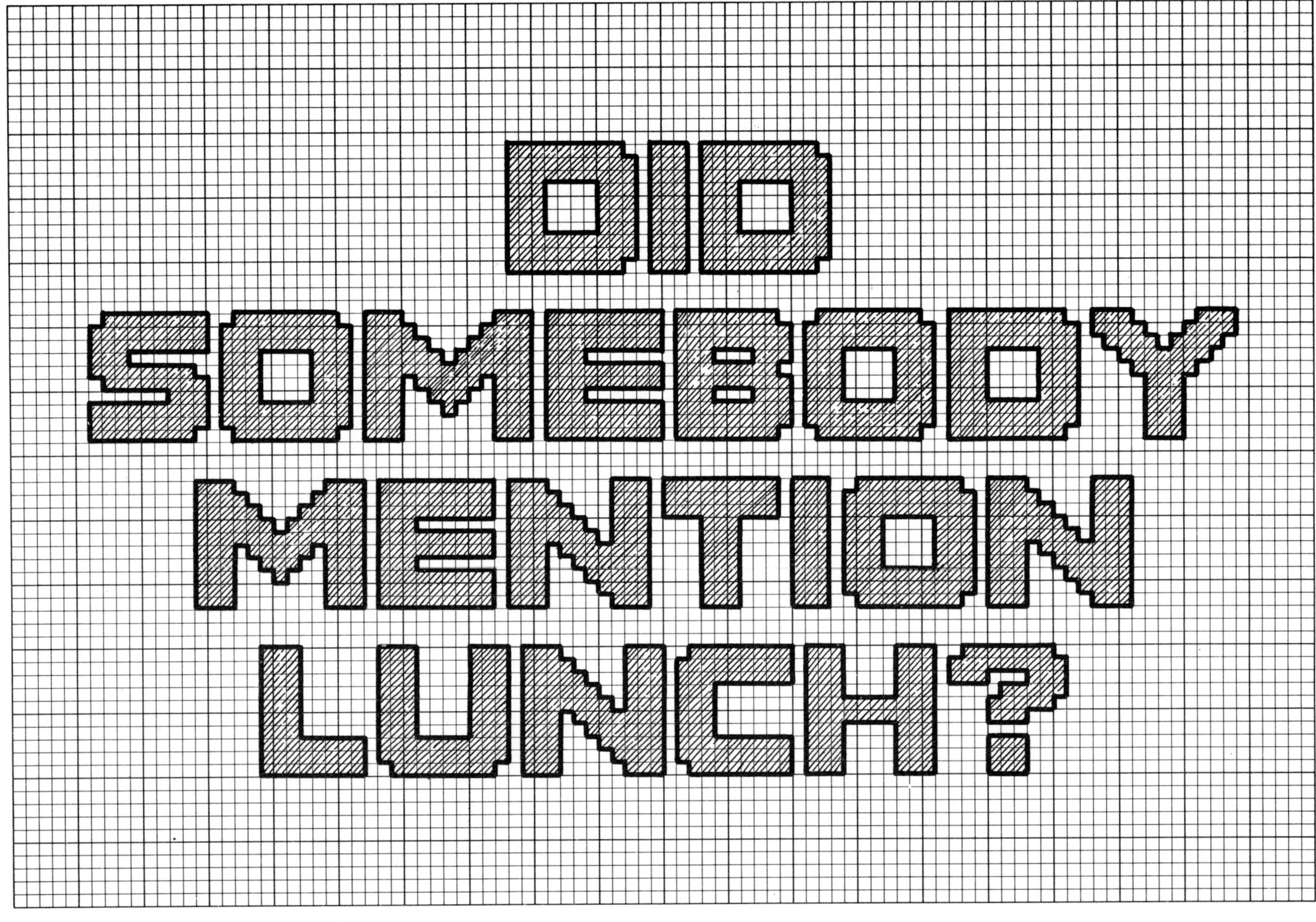
DID
SOMEBODY
MENTION
LUNCH?

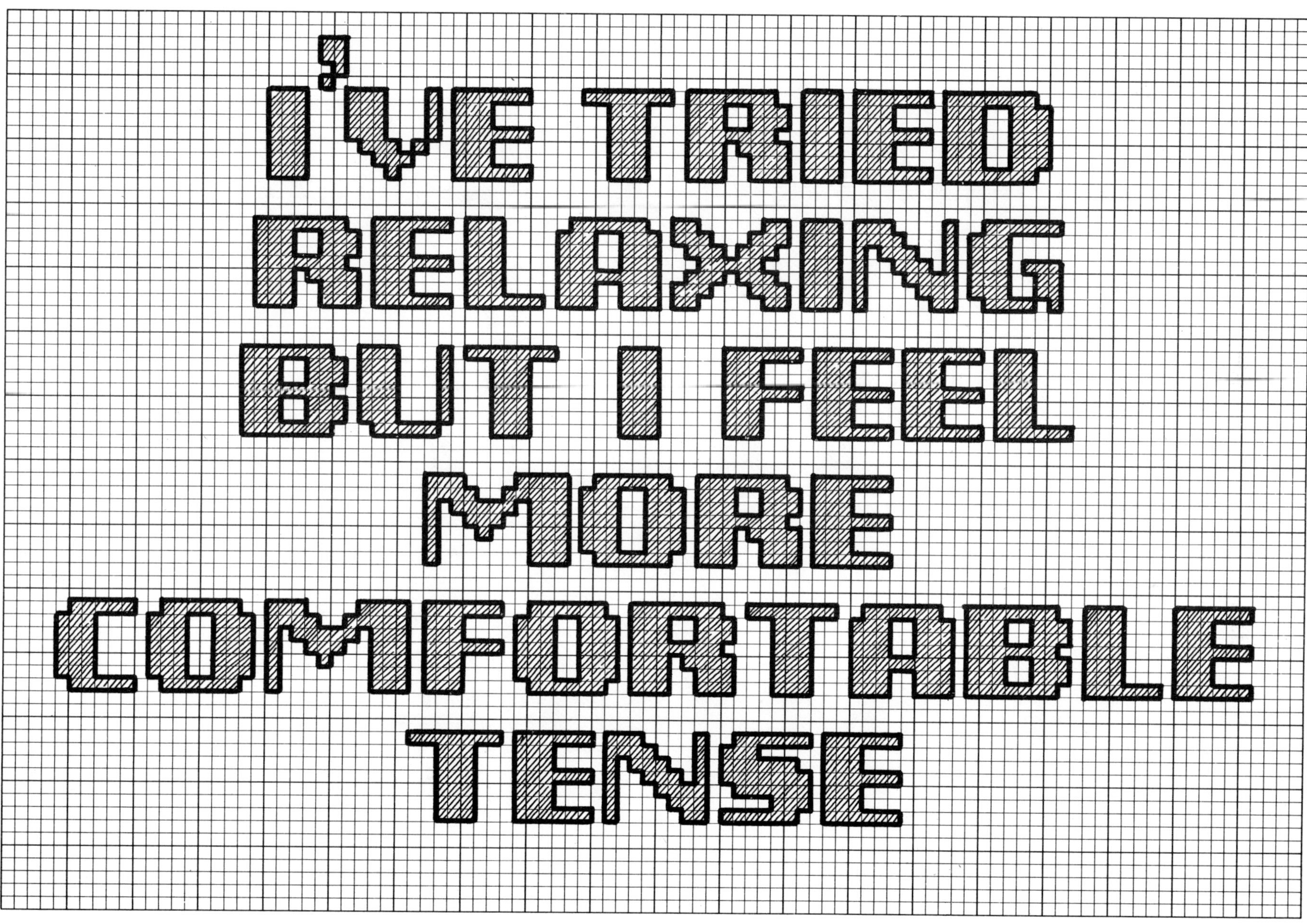
I'VE TRIED
RELAXING
BUT I FEEL
MORE
COMFORTABLE
TENSE

LIVING WELL
IS THE BEST
REVENGE

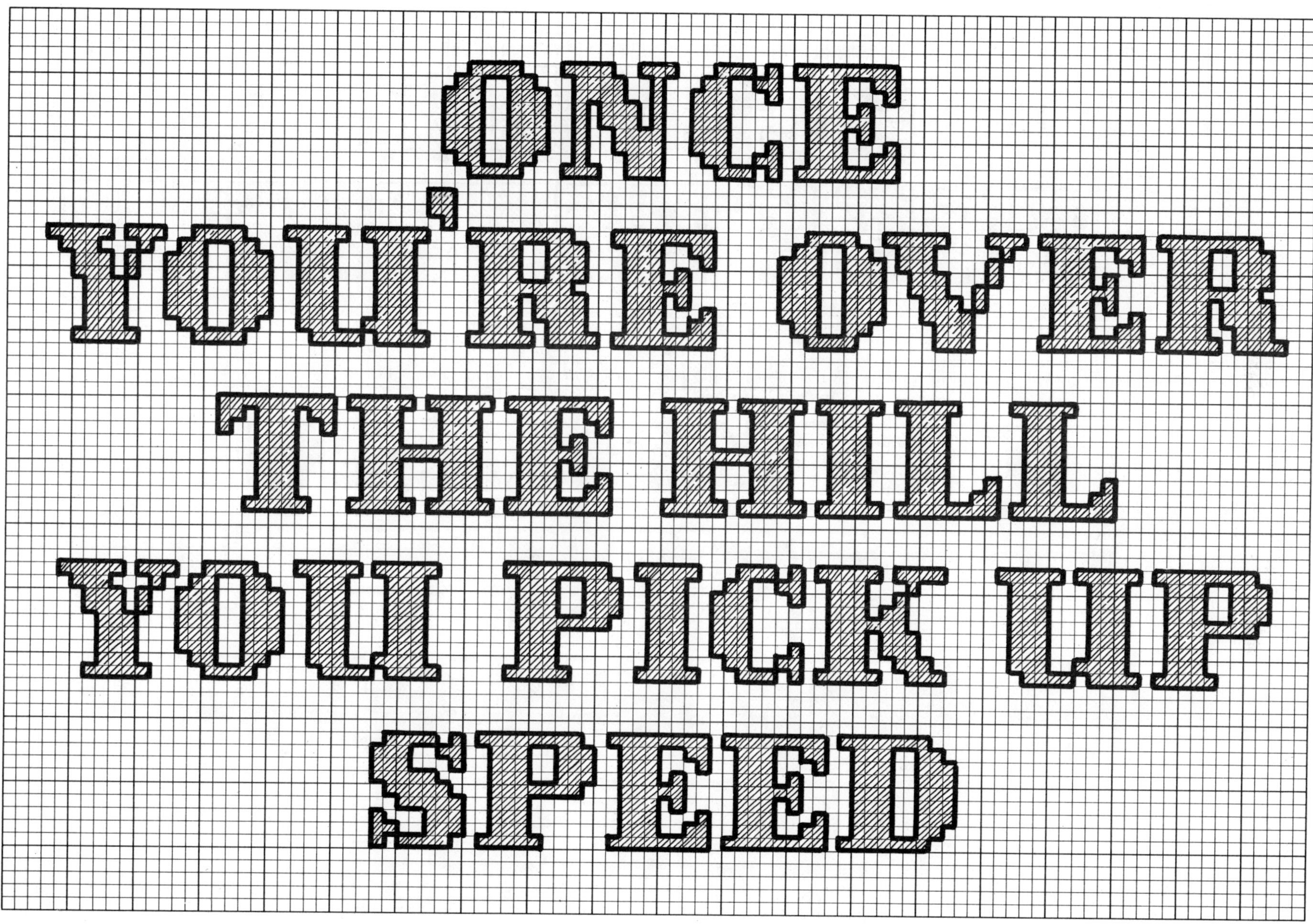
ONCE
YOU'RE OVER
THE HILL
YOU PICK UP
SPEED